WORK – PRISON OR PLACE OF DESTINY?

Work
Prison or Place of Destiny?

DAVID OLIVER

WORD PUBLISHING

WORD ENTERTAINMENT LTD
Milton Keynes, England

WORK – PRISON OR PLACE OF DESTINY?

First edition published 1999 by Word Publishing,
a division of Word Entertainment Ltd, 9 Holdom Avenue,
Bletchley, Milton Keynes, Bucks, MK1 1QR, UK.

ISBN 1-8602-4340-1

Produced for Word Publishing by
Bookprint Creative Services, P.O. Box 827, BN21 3YJ, England.
Printed in Great Britain.

CONTENTS

Foreword   7
Dedication   9
A Personal Note   10
Introduction – No I haven't commited adultery!   11
  1. From Swanage to Auschwitz   15
  2. Overview and Trends   20
  3. The Church Could Be There   30
  4. Prison or Destiny? It Depends on What You Believe   39
  5. Prison or Destiny? The Big Lie   47
  6. Six Months Without Pay!   56
  7. God's Anvil   67
  8. Watch Out For the Wolf   75
  9. Supporting the Church With Work-Based Skills   85
10. Reflecting Reality in Our Churches   94
11. Sex   106
12. Money!   121
13. Gifts and Ministries in the Workplace   128
14. Three Homosexuals and a Lady Called Margaret
    Thatcher   140
15. A Stone's Throw   153
16. Discipling Men and Women in The World of Work   165
17. Radical Repackaging and Stuck Churches   171
18. Champagne for God   179
19 How to Eat This Elephant   191

6　　　　　　　　　　　CONTENTS

Appendix I　Where to Now? – Working Men and
　　　　　　Women　　　　　　　　　　　　　194
Appendix II　Where to Now? – Church Leaders and
　　　　　　Leadership Teams　　　　　　　　205
Appendix III　References　　　　　　　　　　　208
Appendix IV　Bibliography　　　　　　　　　　211
Appendix V　Topics for Preaching and Teaching　213
Appendix VI　Foundations for a Business　　　　215

Services and Resources from David Oliver for Churches
　and Businesses　　　　　　　　　　　　　　217

FOREWORD

Packed into a Nairobi hotel room, one hundred and fifty Kenyan Christian working men and women ate their way through a pleasant meal and prepared to listen to the speaker for the evening.

Some expected to be preached at, to give more for the work of the Church; others expected to be told they weren't doing enough in the Church. A few, more seasoned, were mentally preparing to 'ward off' any such approach. The speaker stood and totally shocked them as he quietly put tools into their hands, 'Secrets of the Kingdom' which would improve their business yields, insights that would develop their world and please their Saviour and all at no financial cost!

David Oliver then went on to open their minds with the truth of God's Word and in an encouraging manner, envisioned and affirmed to them that work was their godly calling.

Many times I have had the privilege of hearing Dave do this with Kingdom workers in many countries. He is a passionate man, with a burning desire to give Christians a sense of destiny, purpose and support in the workplace. An awareness of being ambassadors for Christ and a sense of being 'salt and light' in the community flow from him. His own marketing and consultancy activities have always benefited from his clear understanding of the Word of God. As an elder in the Basingstoke

7

Community Church, Dave has encouraged many to see they are not second-class to the pastors, but carry a vital role into society. His dynamism inspires and his human vulnerability ensures others can approach him and learn as much from his mistakes as from his successes. From sophisticated Swedes to Neolithic Aboriginals, people have benefited from his counsel. Dave is at home in this area and encourages many to find God's heavenly workplace for themselves.

I am thrilled that Word have published his work. I believe it is long overdue that the Church recognises its members in the workplace and support them in a more credible and validating way. I foresee a change in 'doing church' – where the Church supports its workers not the workers the Church – and I believe David Oliver is one of those equipped by God to help the Church make this paradigm shift into the new millennium.

As a friend, co-worker and his pastor I recommend this book to you and trust it will dramatically improve your life, your calling, your work.

May the Kingdom of God come in the workplace!

Dave Richards
Salt & Light Ministries
Spring Harvest
E.A. Council of Reference

DEDICATION

To my family

You are a hard working family and I love you. It is very special to me to see my wife and children hard at work in some chosen sphere or other. That is probably one of the most meaningful things I could experience. Thank you each of you for seeing the value of work and giving yourselves to it.

Thank you too for often releasing me into the call of work when it takes me places. And thank you for catching the Spirit's vision and beginning to fly with it for yourselves.

A PERSONAL NOTE

A word of introduction. I am a husband, a father of four children, a church leader and a working man. In the course of my life I have worked on the shop floor, and have been employed in a whole variety of office jobs from clerical to senior management. I now run two companies – an international training and consultancy organisation and a recruitment company. I will refer to a number of my own experiences throughout the book not because I am some kind of 'good boy' but simply because the message of this book is inextricably linked with those experiences and in that sense I would like you to share in the reality of the joys and the pain, the successes and the weaknesses.

Basingstoke Community Church has been my home church for over 20 years. During that time the church has grown from 70 adults to well over 700. The leadership team has been incredibly supportive of the concepts we will look at together and they have been an integral part of the journey that the book reflects. On a number of occasions either I or the church, or both, have got work-related things wrong – even seriously wrong.

It may be that occasionally you will feel the personal or church references are a little intrusive, but please bear with me as we share our failures and occasional successes.

INTRODUCTION

No, I haven't committed adultery!

Fifteen years ago, my wife Gill and I had the children looked after while we travelled to Bognor Regis and borrowed her parents' static caravan for a weekend away. We were into weekends away but this one was different. No romantic meals, no trips out! What were we doing there? We were listening to twelve hours of tapes on the Kingdom of God and we didn't want to leave until we had devoured that material and allowed it to change our lives. Little did we know what the Word of God would do and how it would dramatically change the course of our lives.

I had been preaching, even back then, about the place of work in the Christian world. Dennis Peacock had already lit our fires more than a little, but with one or two exceptions the Church by and large, and church leadership in particular, seemed more or less uninterested.

What a change in the last few years! This March I was invited, for the first time ever, to do sessions on 'The Kingdom of God at Work' in King's Bible College. In 1998 Spring Harvest had their first ever Christian leaders' conference aimed at working leaders and church leaders (Sheffield – 'At Work Together'). I was privileged and excited to be invited to be part of that experience.

In the last few years alone I have been invited again and again to talk about 'The Kingdom of God and Work' in the UK, in Kenya, in Sweden, in Zimbabwe, in the USA and in India. It is as if the prophetic word voiced in its infancy nearly two decades ago is starting to take hold. The mustard seed of revelation is growing into a tree that will fill the whole earth. In this area of life it may just be that the Kingdom of God is coming of age.

But back to Bognor! What was it that so dramatically changed our lives? Gill and I had always assumed we had the magical so-called 'full-time' call to ministry. Various supernatural encounters had postured us towards what we thought was our calling. We were travelling all over the place preaching and trying to move increasingly in the prophetic realm. We saw a full-time ministry as working primarily for and into the Church, but that weekend and what followed was where our eyes opened. A new horizon opened up, the possibility that our ministry could be equally shared in the world of work and the world of the Church. Even that, in time, would change again as our theology gradually got challenged, shaped and moulded. We would see in time that our ministry, our calling, was a seamless whole. God did not divide it into either compartment.

So here I am writing a book for Word about the world of work. I have been an apprentice on the shop floor, worked as a church-paid staff member, been a clerk in an office, a manager in large and small family-owned businesses, and more recently, in the last eleven years, have run Insight Marketing, a company which specialises in training worldwide in marketing, sales, negotiation and leadership development. I think since the Bognor weekend we have trained over 50,000 individuals. I understand the pressures of work on the shop floor, I understand the tremendous privileges of being employed and the many frustrations that it can bring. I know what it is to run a company with all the blessings and tensions that it involves. But more than all of that I do believe that, in a way probably unique in world history, working men and women today have a chance to see the Kingdom of God expressed in our generation on a scale not experienced before.

I haven't taken up this role because I fell morally, hence the title of this chapter. I haven't taken this up because I can't make it as church leader. I live this because it is God's breath in me, God's word, God's direction and God's high calling. And I am in this because my fellow elders and leaders in Basingstoke Community Church have loved me, encouraged me and helped me begin to discover with them what 'The Kingdom of God at Work' really means.

So why write this book? That question is a bit like asking a pregnant woman why she is giving birth. I feel so full of this revelation. It's not mine, it's not original, but I do feel in seminated with it. It's been steadily growing and it is probably ready to pop out of the womb. Terry Nahiry, a student at King's Bible College said this:

> I was greatly **challenged** to view my whole theology of work differently. I was very **encouraged** with the teaching on us being created to work and to work wholeheartedly. I felt **something break** in me during the teaching. I feel more **released** to put everything into my jobs back home. I now feel like I've robbed my employers of what the Kingdom is, because I for some reason placed ministry in the Church above ministry in society.

If this book could **challenge**, **encourage** and **release** you, I would be delighted, whether you are a church-paid ministry, a businessman, a shop-floor worker or someone in vocational calling. May God bless you as you open up your hearts and minds. In fact would you do me a favour? Before you start the next chapter, would you pray one of those quick, 'on-the-hoof' prayers and ask God to challenge, encourage and release you? Would you be good enough to do that now? Thanks.

Chapter 1

FROM SWANAGE TO AUSCHWITZ

Let me tell you three brief personal stories to help you understand where I'm coming from.

I remember sitting on Swanage pier when Joel my eldest son was five or six. As we sat there with our crab lines dangling far below in the water, hauling up the unfortunate prospects, something else unforgettable was taking place. Joel's attention was not on the crabbing but he was counting the number of people with crab lines. 'Dad, how much money do you think it cost to make those crab lines? How much did they sell them for?' He spent the next few minutes trying to calculate how much the manufacturers had made on this one day's transactions. It was unforgettable, not in some dramatic way but simply that he had begun to explore, at an incredibly early age, the principles of supply and demand, the principles of a wholesome product or not, the enjoyment of the customer and the issue, the alluring issue, of profit. It was unforgettable for me as a Dad because I saw the future for him. I saw just a glimpse that day of what God had made him to be.

Twelve years later, Joel and I were visiting Auschwitz and Berkenhau assessing the horrific impact of the holocaust. Looking into the ovens that had scorched and charred fathers, mothers, sons and daughters, from the same families, to grey ash. Looking at other exhibits of scene after scene of human misery, one of the things that struck us with incredible power was the fact that the Nazi perpetrators ran the whole thing as a business. Even to the grisly details of selling gold fillings and human hair. Gold that would find its way into the cynical banks of Switzerland or even our own Barclays Bank in Paris! Human hair that was sent off to line the suits of the rich, or alternatively as upholstery material on German furniture. Working out in great detail the maths of production, the ways to greater efficiency. It was as if the evil could somehow be covered by the routine, the normality and the pleasure of business principles. I remember the very strange feelings running through my own mind as I looked at the exhibits in the various rooms at Auschwitz, and saw many corporate names, names such as AEG, Bata, IG Farben, Krupp, Portland Zement and Siemens. Now I am sure that these corporations have changed since then, but how could respectable household names such as BMW (I even drive their cars) participate in a business venture with such horrific implications? I don't know if we will ever answer those questions satisfactorily.

The salt mine

The contrast for Joel and I was marked when we visited the Wieliczka salt mine just one day later, located only a few miles away. Several thousand feet below ground, we witnessed one of the most wholesome and motivating business set-ups I have ever seen. Salt mining, rather like coal mining, can be viewed as unpleasant, hazardous, dark and unfriendly, but not here. The atmosphere oozed quality and wholesomeness. Horses were treated with respect and were winched up each month, so as to have one month above ground and one month below. The miners were given a hunk of pure salt each week for themselves. The value of that was so high it could be bartered for a wide range of services. Most of the miners were trained in sculpturing and in their spare hours they would sculpt out of salt in the underground rock face. What they achieved in their sculpture was truly outstanding. There were statues, story lines told in long friezes along the tunnel walls, but most incredible of all was an underground cathedral, full size with a carved tiled floor. There were statues, including Jesus on the cross and a Christmas scene, all carved impeccably and intricately from the salt deposits in the working areas.

The impact of that is still with me to this day. There was respect for the dignity of humans and animals. There was a share in the product produced and there was a blend of faith with creative and recreational pastimes. There was an incredible level of job satisfaction in what could have been dark, damp and dreary conditions. All that just twenty minutes away from the demonic business principles at the camps.

Why have I begun with these three stories? Well, because they stirred something at the deepest level of my personality. What did I really believe about God and work? What could I learn about the nature of wholesome principles of work? How come I had hardly ever heard a single message in forty-seven years as a Christian – twenty-seven of those as a leader – which really touched the heart of these issues? How come so few Christians really resonate with destiny in the workplace? How come we so often feel guilty, or are made to feel guilty by inference, when we give large chunks of our time into the working environment? How come so few leaders in churches are men in demanding responsible jobs? And because I am a church leader myself, I found myself asking if today's churches have moved away from their earliest and defining belief in the value and priesthood of all believers. Have we in our churches simply developed a theology of work that in fact devalues everyone not paid from church funds? As you will see I do believe, by and large, we have done exactly that.

This book will inevitably challenge the 'status quo' of working people and church leaders alike. It will challenge our mindset towards the place of work. It will rattle a few cages, not just to be brash or blasé, but because I do believe that God has something to say today to working people. Equally for those of us who are church leaders, pastors and elders, it may just be that God wants to wake us up to sobering realities in this as well as other areas, otherwise, as we will see in chapter ten, the Church will risk becoming even more irrelevant to the reality of contemporary life.

A vasectomy reversed

One of the great victories of Satan in recent decades has been to get the Church lying on the operating table of uncertainty whilst his surgeon's knife removes the sterile elements of the womb of the Body of Christ. He has tied the tubes. I get angry at this. My cry is, 'God, let the Church have her reproductive vitality again!'

Satan has sold us the great lie, and we have progressively swallowed his bait and given over the world of work to the non-Christian world. My prayer is that, as men and women are exposed to the growing prophetic sound, an awakening will emerge. Men and women will seize the Kingdom by force in the world of work and vocation. Let the trumpet sound, let the hearts of our generation be stirred. God is on the move, and on the move in the world of work. Teachers, doctors, nurses, policemen, lawyers, engineers, dinner ladies, shop-floor workers, craftsmen, if you will hear it, the Prince of Life wants to walk with you, sweep with you, care with you, teach through you, become entrepreneurial with you.

Freedom from guilt

I remember one of my friends, Niall Barry, said to me one day, 'You know you have His permission to be successful; you have His blessing to be successful'. I was, and am, so grateful for those words, but what an indictment that they should ever be necessary. I have met thousands of men and women who somehow feel less than spiritual, even guilty, because they are working day after day in a non-church environment. I have met many who can't really enjoy it because of various beliefs and pressures. I have met others who are so restless, so dissatisfied, so frustrated because they can't see a way out of the prison of work. I want the words of my friend to be words of comfort and challenge. Wherever you are, as you read this, reach out and sense His pleasure, His appointing, His anointing. Could you dare to believe that when you go to work you are fulfilling a destiny written into the software of your life from heaven's programming department? Could you dare to believe this is what you were created for? If you could believe that, what difference would it make? Destiny! Just about every Christian you speak to is looking for the thing that God has apprehended them for. Suppose this is it? Yes, you and your job with your customers, your machines, your patients.

Where are your wings?

Where are your wings? Our family was walking around Birdworld in the USA. We passed one area where, huddled and shrinking away in the darkness of some conifer bushes, there was a majestic Golden Eagle. The children were dismayed. Here was the most magnificent of all birds held into a dark corner of the world by a small chain holding it to a log. One of the boys wanted to jump into the enclosure and set the thing free, and had to be restrained.

All over the Christian world there are chained eagles. Logs of false teaching, chains of false expectation and false doctrine, holding down some magnificent men and women who deep down are longing to fly. Longing for permission, for understanding, for conviction. Longing to feel the wind of the Spirit blow under outstretched wings as they get lifted into the thermals high up in God's purpose. The time is here, the place is now. As you read, will you let the word of God break those chains? Will you let His Spirit breathe into your faint hope, your faint faith and let Him stir you up, lift you up, to something higher?

Chapter 2

OVERVIEW AND TRENDS

Before we explore vision and examine our attitudes towards work I want to paint a brief overview of the world of work as it is today.

Over the next six years we can expect the pace of change in society to accelerate. Here are some areas which will affect church life and working life for most of us as we cross into the next millennium. I wonder if we are ready for their impact!

1. A Seven Day Society

This will raise all kinds of questions and pressures for Christians in the workplace. There is a growing blur between the week and the weekend. Those who are working full-time, particularly in the UK, and particularly male employees, have the longest average working week in the European Union. The school week of Monday to Friday may keep a partial brake on the trend, but the trend is nonetheless there. I watch with interest my own irritation when the Post Office closes on Saturday at noon, or when the florist isn't open on Sundays, when I would like to take a bunch of flowers to someone in the church. My irritation, whilst certainly not godly, is an indication of what we have come to expect in terms of service levels and service frequency.

Implications. Many of those in normal working employment are already feeling the tiredness and stress associated with long and uncertain hours. This means many have already decided they are too tired to contribute to church events during the week. As the number of people working on Sundays increases, churches will have to think through alternative meeting patterns. This will probably need more thought and prayer than simply providing a service at a different time.

2. Continued Globalisation of Society

Technology and the philosophies behind it mean that many companies – even small companies – view their markets as global. You could buy this book from Amazon books anywhere in the world. Some years back I was in the remotest part of the jungles of Borneo, when floating down the river came a Coke bottle. I have never yet found it impossible to buy a Coke anywhere in the world. Branded trainers, for example, are indispensable in Lusaka as well as London, as common in townships as they are in tower blocks.

Implications. Even small business start-ups can access the power of globalisation by using e-mail and the Internet. There are also major opportunities for the worldwide church to work together and speak together. If there are, as reported, 1.8 billion Christians, that is an incredible amount of pressure group activity. Just this last week I was e-mailed and asked to vote for Jesus as the most popular man of the millennium on *'Time'* magazine's news site. When I registered my vote, Jesus already had 46% of the vote!

3. Increased Fragmentation of Society

It seems that in most countries the rich are getting richer and the poor are getting poorer. Culture gaps are getting wider rather than narrowing. This is reflected in the types of work available to the 'have nots'.

Implication. The Church in the UK is over represented by 'middle class, white, suburban England'. One of the ways in which we can adjust this is by changed attitudes towards work and towards the way our church activity reaches these different groupings.

4. Increased Flexibility in Working Patterns

In the western world the trend towards different, less rigid forms of working practice is having an impact and this will increasingly be the case. '*The Daily Telegraph*', 4 March 1999, cites one forecast suggesting that in twenty years time, 50% of white collar workers will be part-time or self-employed. Another study relates the following:

Figure 1: UK Employees' work patterns

	Work Part-Time	Temporary Work	Flexible Work hours	Term-time Working	Home Working
1985	20.9%	5.6%	—	—	—
1995	26.2%	7.1%	10.1%	4.0%	2.6%
2005	29.1%	9.2%	10.8%	4.2%	5.3%

Implication. As differing types of working pattern emerge, traditional hours will disappear and Christians may be willing to become involved in their churches in very different ways and at very different times. This can have an impact, either providing less income or providing time for additional self-employment.

5. Emerging Technology

The power available in home computers is increasing at an exponential rate. I have two PC's and a laptop at home. Any one of those, on its own, has far greater computing power than the computers which put the Apollo rockets on the moon! We are told that by the year 2005 home computers will have speeds of 5000 mhz, compared with 450 mhz today. They are far more likely to be aware of their surroundings through increased video and voice recognition. At home, at work and during our leisure time, the frequency and depth of our interaction with computers can be expected to increase significantly.

A recent radio news clip suggested that children starting school today need hardly bother with such IT skills as keyboard entry. Why? Because in their generation, and even fairly soon, computers should become voice-activated.

Implication. Whatever work we do, we will need to be familiar with IT. We would also do well to think creatively about how this power can be useful to us at home as well as at church and work.

6. Internet Growth

By 2005 we can expect over 80% of homes in the UK to be connected to the Internet. Current rate of growth in Internet usage is about 80% per annum (Source – *NOP Internet User Profile Survey*). Home usage doubled between Dec 96 and Dec 97 from 0.86m to 1.9m. In March 99 the Finnish Press carried an article estimating that over half the population had an active connection to the Internet. So it's official, Internet business is very definitely growing and will continue to grow at an increasing rate.

Spending on Internet access across Europe will reach £7 billion by the year 2002, from an estimated £1.5 billion this year. Consumer spending is estimated to be only 40% of that market. What that means is that, if these trends are accurate, the increase will come from the working world.

- 28m users in 1996
- 50m users in 1997
- 90m users in 1998

One of my clients, First Index (an on-line directory) has seen its Internet access grow from 3000 hits per **month** to just under 1000 hits per **day** in the last six months! A recent survey in the UK said that 46% of all buyers are on e-mail or the Net. The Economist said, 'The Internet will almost certainly have a stronger impact than the PC. A reasonable guess might even put it ahead of the telephone and the television.'

Implication. For anyone in work, the Internet is a marvellous source of information and resource. It is also a useful and cost-effective marketing medium for businesses when understood properly. The Internet is a major opportunity for evangelism – both globally and locally. It offers total freedom of communication around the world. Its impact on the family needs to be evaluated and harnessed, as pornography, violence and unrestricted access to knowledge is at the fingertips of our pre-teens. And believe me they know how to find it!

7. Stress at Work

   58% of people fear losing their job
   63% are under more stress than 5 years ago
   44% have trouble sleeping
   26% drink more
   60% are exhausted
   56% have no time for family or relations
   (Source – *NOP poll of 1003 employed persons*)

Serious stress is developing in our nation. Many of those who are in work are being worked harder and harder for longer hours. A recent survey showed that in Britain the percentage of men working over 46 hours per week is 42%, the highest in Western Europe. In Germany it is 14%.

Implications. This is having an effect on our churches as attendance at mid-week events declines. It has a direct relationship to what we believe, in terms of work itself, rest and stewardship of time.

8. Fewer Quality Relationships

This is one of the decade's hidden problems. The UK *BBC News* on 19th April 99 commissioned a survey and discovered that the average person in 1999 has only three close friends, in contrast with say ten years ago when the number was six.

The reasons given were twofold;

1. that people are changing jobs, even careers, at an increasing rate – one commentator reckoned every two to three years.
2. time constraints at work, where there are increasing demands, put a strain on existing relationships and offer less time to develop existing or foster new ones.

The outcome is what one sociologist called semi-detached functional friends. Of course services such as date-line and computer matching become alarmingly commonplace as the means for effecting an environment by which we can meet potential friends. Electronic friendship has become another 90's norm. Instead of catching a bus or driving to see someone, we spend a few seconds typing in some cute comments, press a button and communicate. E-mail has in this sense become a substitute for friendship.

Implications. Real friendships and communication at work and in the Church could be dangerously undermined with the overuse of e-mail. One wise church leader has asked his leaders not to relate by e-mail for this very reason. The lack of friends

is serious in its implications for evangelism. Jesus was the friend
of sinners – it seems we may not have time to be!

9. Network Marketing Models of Business

There is a large increase in the number of companies offering
this kind of income generation. The principle is to provide you
with an opportunity for a business start up with little or no risk
and no capital requirement. The idea relies on your ability to
get a number of individuals working for you, providing an
ongoing base of income. Your success is dependent on their
success, which in turn means that you will work hard to help
those individuals and ensure that they are successful. The
company Amway has been doing this very effectively for some
years; more recently, in the Christian world, a vitamin supple-
ment company, Usana, has approached a number of my friends
and colleagues.

The growth of network marketing is quite substantial. In
North America there are well over 7 million distributors – that
is 2.4% of the population. Canada and Mexico have similar
percentages. Australia and New Zealand have 2.7% of their
population engaged in network marketing. Edward Ludbrook,
in his book *The Big Picture*, predicts that, 'Network Marketing
in the UK will involve 1.2 million people turning over £1.8
billion worth of products by the year 2000.'

Implications. There are some potentially dangerous side-effects.
A number of times when the concept has been put to me, the
line has been that this is a way to make money and free up time
for the Church. This, as we shall see, does not represent God's
view of work. Also, church people will often go to other church
people as their network. That, in my view, is an inappropriate
use of the relationships we have in the Body of Christ. I am sure
that is not what is in the minds of the founders, but it can very
easily be present in the outworking.

Having said that, there are some excellent applications where the Church is not used and where a genuinely beneficial product is provided.

10. Uncertain Times

Let me quote how one consultancy, Teleios, have approached uncertain times. Teleios is a group of businessmen and women who share a common faith and a passion to make a difference in the market place. They say:

> To say that we are living in uncertain times seems a wonderfully understated comment, given all that is going on in our small world. We are experiencing massive political, technological, biological, and economic changes, with consequences we can only guess at. I suspect, despite the illusion of certainty and progress offered by the guru's crystal ball, most of us in business feel we are on a roller coaster ride, never quite sure which way is up.
>
> It is against this background that leaders still need to lead, managers to manage, sales people to sell, people to be increasingly effective in their unique roles. Common to all markets in all parts of the world is the pressure to produce more from less. Although this is not new, set against the information revolution that is going on all around, it is producing unparalleled stresses, tensions and indeed opportunities. This truly is the drama of life.
>
> It is in this drama that we see the forces of heroism and complacency, hope and fear, materialism and high idealism at work in countless lives. What a time for us as Christians to be salt and light; what a time to see ministry as a service to the world not just to the Church!

> *Implications.* We have the privilege of working with organisations big and small throughout Europe and the USA. In our various roles as trainers, coaches, catalysts and change agents, we daily come face to face with people at their point of need. We have had the tremendous thrill of seeing significant breakthroughs, we have also sat with people who have lost all sense of hope and shared their tears.

We come across many Christians in business who are doing an incredible job living their faith at the cutting edge. It's great to encourage each other. We work too with a greater number who do not share our beliefs, but are intrigued by seeing the principles of our faith working in the market place. We try and leave these people with some interesting questions. We share our faith, hopefully in ways that are appropriate, and sometimes we share just a cup of water. It really is a thrill to serve our customers and friends, in whatever way we can. We were made and commissioned for such a time as this.

Business, and indeed many parts of academia, are really searching for answers, not knowing quite what questions to ask. There is a real openness and inquisitiveness and although some of this is promoted by the pragmatic need to produce more from less, the openness remains. This is the territory we need as Christians to occupy, and the great news is, many, many people are doing just that.

11. Constant Change

Let me quote from Teleios again:

> Whether it is a large multinational company or a charity, we find that people are searching for real answers to life's dilemmas. Some of that searching is pragmatic – 'How do we get more from less?' 'How do we lead and manage in complex global organisations?' 'How do we manage change?'
>
> And some of it goes deeper and touches at the heart of the human dilemma. 'I have climbed the corporate ladder and stand at the top. Is this it?' 'How do I cope with doing three people's work, and be a good father and have time for me?' 'I am tired, stressed, well paid and asking what it is all about.'

Implications. Many within our profession (organisation, management and learning consultants) draw on ancient ideologies and esoteric sources to help people. We believe that there is a tremendous opportunity for us as Christians to take our place on this battlefield and, as best we can, demonstrate the Christian message in practice.

Our belief is that 'life in all its fullness' can only come through Christ. What we present are Biblical principles in the language of the market place. When people see how well these principles work, some ask where they come from and this opens up another conversation. We don't preach, but try to be 'salt and light' for those we work with.

All the staff in Teleios have worked at senior levels of business and all have been recognised by their professions as having made a difference to current thinking and practice. Various books and published articles use their work as benchmark examples of best practice and several of the team work for Cranfield University and Business School. They are a marvellous model for the next chapter, *'The Church Could Be There'*.

Summarising these areas of change we could safely say, 'We do not have a New World order but a troubled and fractured planet' (Peter Kennedy). Identity crumbles as society fails, religious groups provide a source of identity and a social community to work it out. What a time for the Church to offer an alternative! What a time for the Church to be there!

Chapter 3

THE CHURCH COULD BE THERE

As we have just read, society is on the move in all kinds of ways. Change is almost at epidemic levels – think of the changes in large company mergers such as BMW and Rover, or Wal-Mart's takeover of Asda. God's people – the Church – could be right there, there is no better group on the face of the earth to handle such a time on the planet. The Bible offers clearly defined models of leadership with flexible applications.

In a recent report from Ashridge Management College, fifty managers aged between 36 and 40 stated that they wanted an empowering risk-taking environment which encourages innovation and has a clear sense of purpose. The leadership may pass from one to another as a project progresses.

Today, people are likely to pass in and out of leadership roles. Think about it for a moment. This kind of approach to leadership rings a bell, doesn't it? Think about the kind of teamwork Jesus and the disciples modelled. It is the kind of model which Jesus intended the Christian church to grow by.

In this time of incredible and rapid change, what the Kingdom of God has to offer is so appropriate and relevant. However, as a whole, the Church is probably not aware of the opportunities that really do exist. As I write this, to all intents and purposes we are at war with Serbia. Three American soldiers have been abducted and paraded on TV in a typical Milosovic propaganda coup. I find tremendous anger welling up inside, and my thoughts turn to the SAS, wishing they were in place. History has shown that it takes an infantry company of about 120 armed soldiers to take out four of our SAS troops. What aptitude, what training! Who better to do the job? One calculation states that it costs around £1 million to train each SAS troop.

I have similar feelings about the world of work and God's people, His Church. All the changes we have looked at, all the changes exploding and imploding around us in the world of work, are calling for the crack troops of this generation. This morning I received an invitation to address the Gateway High School in Harare, Zimbabwe. Let me quote what they have asked me to consider;

a) It would not be appropriate to have a sermon or a purely theoretical dissertation
b) What is said must be relevant to both the students and parents
c) A major concern of our parents is how well we are pre-paring our students to face the outside world with high levels of unemployment and an economy in crisis
d) The question that may be asked is, 'How can my child succeed in such an environment?' or in very blunt terms, 'What makes my child marketable?'

What an invitation, and what a clear description of how many view the world today!

I believe that the Church holds the people, holds the answers, holds the way forward and holds hope. We really could be the SAS of the working world if we would see the training and knowledge that we really do have. We are the prepared ones, are we not? Of all people on this planet we know the truth, we believe in absolutes (which work in the business world), we understand how to overcome fear, insecurities and relational problems. We understand love and care and the concept of customer service. But above all that, we are probably the most equipped people ever to handle change.

What am I saying? We, the Church, have been prepared for such a time as this. We have the truth that could make us relevant – so relevant – to a hungry, thirsty working world. We, the Church, have been trained in the basic ingredients of constant change, of exposed insecurities.

What about the dramatic and controversial move of the Holy Spirit since 1994? It is said that in the last 25 years we have read more, seen more and experienced more of the Holy Spirit than in the rest of recorded church history added together. One scholar estimated that of all the books written on the Holy Spirit and His gifts, nearly 90% have been written in the last 30 years.

Like it or not, charismatic or not, the Holy Spirit has done something truly unique on a global scale in our generation. In fact, even the move of the Spirit since 1994 has equipped us uniquely for change in a way that non-Christians simply cannot emulate. What has it done? What is it for? Come on now, pentecostal or reformed anti-charismatic, please answer the question. Well, it's certainly not so that we can debate yet again speaking in tongues. It's not so that we can laugh or fall on the floor. I have done all those things; they have value, but on their own they do little and lead nowhere. Could it be that it has been the sound of the bridegroom coming? The sound of Prince Charming kissing the Sleeping Beauty to wake her up to her responsibilities, to rule, to govern, to reign. To bring answers, kindness, justice and love to the subjects of the kingdom of love.

If only we the Church would wake up! It's time to get walking, so we have less athlete's foot to pray over in our cell groups. It's time to take our lampshade off, and maybe, just maybe, we could be the light of the world in BMW/Rover, in the NHS trusts, in the state school system, on the shop floor. It's time to lay down some of our own thoughts and prejudices and

be shaken like the salt of the earth into the working institutions of our planet. Maybe then we really would heal, sting, preserve and bring flavour to our hurting sick, apathetic, rotting society.

I have met hundreds of leaders trained by the churches in the last few years. Men and women who run cell groups, teach, prophesy or pastor small churches. Many of these are SAS quality, frontline elite. If only, somehow, the same church groups that train them, could release them into the wider world instead of sucking their talents into ever increasing – and sometimes increasingly more irrelevant – meetings.

They are so trained up, some of them are fidgety with pent-up energy. Come on church leaders, how about sending out some of your best? Send them out in twos if you can, hold them accountable, encourage them, give them unrelenting approbation and give them ten years or more to let their two talents become four and their five become ten. Let the world of work hear their words, see their tears, feel their love and experience the power of God at work through them. The Quakers saw it in a previous generation – ask Rowntree, Nestlé, Coleman, Jarrolds and others.

Of all the generations that have lived on the planet we have surely been most blessed. Blessed with teaching, blessed with the Holy Spirit, blessed with resources. Will we see this window of opportunity and change our thinking, change our church structure and release our church people to fulfil the high calling of God at work?

As the mustard seed grows into the tree, let's not make it into a bonsai. Will we keep clipping away with church focus at its roots, buds and branches? Will we continually try to keep it in our church mould, whatever that is – old, traditional or New Church with its own new liturgy?

Church history has taught us that previous generations have stopped and ultimately died when they stopped embracing change. If we do that, we may unfortunately end up missing the wave!!

A Third Wave Church

Could it be that our church practice won't match the needs of the 21st century working world? Looking at an edited version of James Sculley's management paradigms would suggest that the Church is caught in his 'second wave' –

Second Wave	Third Wave
Hierarchical	Networking
Institutional	Individual
Structured	Flexible
Likes stability	Likes change
Dogmatic	Inspirational
Affordable best	No compromise
To complete	To build

If the Church is built around the second wave, or has leadership models similar to it, then it will fail to be relevant to the average worker on the shop floor, or in the office, hospital, lawyer's practice or whatever. In fact the question must be asked, and sooner or later answered truthfully – does the Church really value state-school teachers, politicians, shop owners, machine shops and hi-tech workers?

When that valuing process is clear, the relevance, and therefore the response, can be quite different. For example, there are specialist church services in the City of London, at St. Helen's, Bishopgate, which regularly draw lunchtime crowds of 500 plus.

On the last Sunday of September last year, Rev. Simon Howard shocked traditionalists by abandoning his church building and holding his harvest festival in the 'fruit & veg' section of his local Asda supermarket in Berkshire. That, I suggest, is a third wave church activity.

The Church and its relevance

Mark Greene a former adman and director of The London Institute of Contemporary Christianity pioneered research

which revealed that in 47% of evangelical churches, congregations consider the teaching to be irrelevant to their everyday lives. Furthermore, when they were asked how well it addresses the issues they face, work scored very poorly.

On a scale of 1 to 4 (where 1 = low relevance and 4 = high relevance), the scores were as follows –

- work   1.68
- home   1.83
- church   2.12
- personal   2.57

If that is true, then the Church is failing to equip us to interact with the world.

In another Mark Greene survey, differing age groups were asked to rate the relevance and trustworthiness of the Church. Those aged 50+ rated the Church as **third** out of thirteen in relevance and trustworthiness. Those aged under 35 rated the Church **bottom** in relevance and trustworthiness.

In a MORI poll reported by *the Daily Telegraph* on 24 March 1999, over half the 16 to 21 year old men and women interviewed said they wanted to run their own businesses and were planning to be millionaires by the time they were 35.

This generation seems to understand the trends we have looked at, and some intend to be a positive part of them. So if the Church is to be there, if the Church is to be relevant, then there will have to be some changes in belief, some changes in practice, some changes in attitude. One of the primary changes will be the answer to the question, 'Who is my neighbour?'

Who is my neighbour?

Julian Sayer, a businessman studying at King's Bible College, wrote the following section as his KBC assignment.

For some time I have struggled with the understandable emphasis by many church leaders to concentrate exclusively upon the advance of God's Kingdom in the immediate locality and the fact that I and the vast majority of members spend 60–70% of our time away from it.

I have been fortunate in that my pastor has worked for me for four years and has a working knowledge of both the industry I work in and the pressures I work under. However, even he is limited in the amount of emphasis he can place on the area outside of his pre-defined geographical responsibility.

We are regularly encouraged to develop relationships with our neighbours, and non-Christian friends. All good stuff, but how much time do we spend with even our closest friend in a month? Probably somewhere between two and ten hours for most of us.

We are encouraged to invite our friends to guest services or events, wash windscreens on a Saturday morning, and sing carols at the old folks' home. All worthwhile and needed, but are we encouraged to witness at work?

In a recent survey of Christians who attend church regularly, seventy-five percent said they had never been asked by their minister about their 'ministry' in their workplace.

Many of us are struggling to develop a relationship with the strange couple next door when our neighbour is just a desk away! However, most church leaders' concerns are related to their immediate neighbourhood and evangelistic activity that will affect the people living there. The vast majority of these programmes encourage us to relate to cold contacts with people we haven't met until we knock on their doors or wash their windscreens. Having lived in the same house for eleven years, and made a consistent effort to get to know the occupants of the ten or so houses in our square, I can testify that it has taken all of that time to build any real quality of relationship with three of them. The others prefer to keep their relationship at arm's length, restricted to a nodding acquaintance at best. Even those with whom we have built friendships adopt what I call the 'So long as it makes you happy' approach to our 'religion', and unless there is a crisis they seem happy enough without God. This is probably because in the short periods of time that we see each other we are both able to hide any struggle we are going through. You can't hide it for very long at work!

The changing nature of work and transport over the last twenty to thirty years now means that many people's strongest relationships are at their place of work, which is often at least thirty miles away. Many of our contacts are 'warm' at work and this is the place where we experience the ups and downs of life, face to face, day by day.

Some church leaders may be excellent at mobilising the Church to 'hit the streets' on a Friday night to hand out soup to the youngsters roaming around, but find it difficult to understand that you felt that taking your colleague, whose wife has just left him, out for a beer was just as important. Maybe that is an extreme situation but it serves to make a point – many Christians have never been encouraged or supported in their efforts to extend the Kingdom of God into their workplace by their pastor, let alone heard any teaching on the area of life which is meant to occupy them six days a week!

There is a significant danger that our church evangelistic strategies are inadvertently designed around getting people into the local church rather than into the Kingdom irrespective of geography. I am not suggesting that there is a deliberate ploy by pastors to build up their ministry or restrict our own, however it seems that the needs of the people in the workplace have never been seriously recognised and addressed.

How does the Church get it so wrong?

The Church gets into trouble whenever it thinks it is in the **Church** business rather than the **Kingdom** business.

In the Church business, people are concerned with church activities, religious behaviour, spiritual things, meetings and cell groups. In the Kingdom business, people are concerned with Kingdom activities, all human behaviour and everything God has made, visible and invisible. Kingdom people see human affairs as saturated with spiritual meaning and Kingdom significance. It is a totally different way of looking at things.

Kingdom people seek first the Kingdom of God and its justice. Church people often put church work above work, above concerns of justice, mercy and truth. Church people think about how to get people into the Church and that is probably why our evangelism is by and large ineffectual. Kingdom people think about how to get the Church into the world. Church people worry that the world might change the Church. They worry about being conformed to this world's mould. Kingdom people work to see the Church change the world.

Church people don't usually like parties, alcohol or bad people. The King of the Kingdom liked all three. When Christians put the Church ahead of the Kingdom, they settle for meetings and they spend increasing amounts of time with the same people. When they catch a vision of the Kingdom of God, their sight shifts to the poor, the orphan, the widow, the refugee, the wretched of the earth and to God's future. They also see with real insight and fresh vision the stressed, the fearful, the hopeless at work and both their heart and their time reach out.

If the Church has one great need, it is this – to be set free for the Kingdom of God, to be set free from the second wave and to become relevant exactly as God intended.

The release to be different at work, and in our churches, depends on our beliefs. It depends on what we truly believe and practice. Is the world of work a tolerated nuisance preventing more church work? Or is it my place of destiny and, if mine, then the Church's place of destiny as well?

Chapter 4

PRISON OR DESTINY?
IT DEPENDS ON WHAT YOU
BELIEVE

What do we think about work? What does God think about it? What does the Bible teach about it? And how does this current move of the Spirit affect it?

When I preach on work, I will often ask the audience, 'How many of you have ever heard a sermon on work?' In nearly every case, it is less than 50%. Until a few years ago, nearly 100% had never heard a sermon on work as a calling. They are startling statistics, because it means that contemporary Christians are not being equipped for the place where they spend 65% of their time.

Is work a tolerated nuisance, or is it the one place in reality where I can most fully express my Christianity? Is work a curse? Is it a trap minimising my ministry? Is it a trap of necessary financial provision? Is it an idol which satisfies my need for meaning, value and self-worth? Or is it a wonderful, challenging, fulfilling and God-given environment?

It depends on what you believe!

What I believe will determine, both in church and place of work, whether I view my work as a place of function or a prison. More importantly, what I believe will determine whether I act as a prisoner or as a motivated steward of life.

39

In this current move of the Spirit, it would be offensive to suggest that this wonderful Holy Spirit with His infinite wisdom, power, creativity and incredible mind is limited, or will limit us, to operating primarily in a church gathering, a church meeting or a church-only context. With all that God has given us, we will probably be the generation that has the biggest opportunity ever given to a single generation. No other generation has had more than we have had, and are still getting.

What do we mean by work? Well, it means the obvious things, like one's job in the office, on the shopfloor, in a factory, working in a hospital or running your own business. It also includes housework – sweeping, cleaning, cooking – it includes studying at college or university, helping with the homework, repairing the plumbing. Work is still work, whether it is paid or unpaid. It includes teaching, emergency services, law and order, social services and the professions.

There is a real danger in what we believe. That danger is to have a mindset that thinks primarily in terms of church activity, church meetings or church function.

Our heroes and our models – our leaders, within the last ten to twenty years have primarily been so called 'full-time' pastors, 'full-time' teachers, 'full-time' evangelists and 'full-time' prophets. I say *'so called'*, because 'full-time' is not a biblical term and yet is a phrase which we use frequently in our kind of circles.

Those that have preached on 'calling' and those that have envisioned us, have in the main been church-employed ministries. But God-given as all those ministries are – and thank God for them – it can leave us with a twisted or distorted view. That view expresses itself in a number of ways – for instance, I am truly approved by God, or I am ultimately recognised, when my gifting and calling is expressed fully within a church context. Perhaps more insidious is the thought that I can only be a real man or woman of God if I am somehow 'full-time'. I would be really anointed, and my gifts would be really validated if I were 'full-time'. Perhaps I could be more pleasing to God, perhaps I could be more effective as a person, perhaps I would be more valuable as an individual, if I were working more in the Church, or for the Church. Nothing could be further from the truth.

Jesus operated in all the gifts of the Spirit – He out-worked His calling – in the market place, in business, on the mountain-side, in homes, with housewives, in fishing, in the legal system, in the street, on water, walking, sailing, playing with children. For every one time He operated in the church building of His day, He used the gifts five to ten times outside that context.

In His parables and stories, He talked about sowers, vineyard workers, harvesters, house-builders, women sweeping the house, bankers, the armed forces. Interestingly enough, there are not many parables about so-called 'full-time' workers!

Few of the Old Testament heroes and models were 'full-time' as we would describe it. The father of our faith, the covenant-bearer Abraham, was a travelling farmer and a businessman. Abraham changed his working practice and his way of life to accommodate God's call. Scripture records that Abraham, Isaac and Jacob dwelt in tents. Why record that? Because their work and lifestyle reflected the call of God on their lives. Moses was both an academic and a nomadic farmer in two phases of his life. Let me ask you a question – *Who was the first prophet in the Bible?* I wonder what name came to your mind. Jesus refers to the first prophet as Abel. Abel was one of scripture's first recorded working men.

Joseph's prophetic ministry began in animal husbandry, took him into service in military households, prison management, and finally into the highest government office.

Ruth fulfilled the purposes of God as a widow, as a refugee and as a housewife. Esther changed the course of world history by auditioning as a beauty queen!

Daniel's great eschatological revelation, concerning the end times, was brought to birth as he worked in the civil service and the king's court. His government job included heading up what was essentially a think tank, developing government policy and providing counsel. His think tank – by the way – included occult strategists!

David was shepherd, poet, musician, military strategist, ruler and harem manager!!

What about the prophets? Amos ran a flock and a sycamore fig grove. Isaiah was in the king's court. Zephaniah was a socialite in court service, with political interest. Ezekiel, whilst coming from a priestly family, was incredibly well-versed in international affairs, culture, shipbuilding and literature. You could call him an *academic*. Nehemiah was a civil-service governor, Obadiah was head of palace management. Elisha was a wealthy landowner with the equivalent of twelve combine-harvesters.

In fact, a quick flip through church history will point out, from a number of commentators, that the demise of the early church's prophetic ministry was attributed in significant part to travelling prophets who expected money from the various congregations that they visited. In other words, they failed precisely because they let go of the world of work.

Jesus himself would have been apprenticed, the senior partner in the family carpentry business. Jesus would almost certainly have dealt with cash flow, pricing, quality, delivery and purchasing. In Mark chapter 6, Jesus is actually referred to as *'the carpenter'*. In fact His life was probably spent from the ages of twelve to thirty working as a tradesman in some capacity. Eighteen years, in contrast with three years on the road teaching and preaching. Jesus knew what it was to work on the shop-floor.

Where do you think Jesus learned his financial skills, his team leadership skills, his ability to handle interpersonal conflict? What about his ability to make impromptu presentations? I can only think of one possible place and that was his eighteen years of work.

By the way, Jesus was probably self-employed – a micro-entrepreneur. I want to challenge you at least to consider that as a possibility. There is a straight-jacket in employment, wholesome though it may be. I would like to stimulate a number of you to become employers – you really do have it in you. Or become self-employed – there are all kinds of flexible and creative options in your walk with God when you do just that.

The biggest surprise of all is that the Old Testament, in the main, was written or dictated by working men who we would say were in 'secular' employment. The Bible is full of examples of God at His work through ordinary men and women. As we have just seen, much of the Old Testament is a record of ordinary men and women at work who were touched by God. It means we can have faith and confidence where we are. Faith to reach out, faith for *more* – not just on Sunday evenings, but every day in our working environments, whatever they are.

As Dennis Peacocke puts it,

> Work is wonderfully godly and eternal. Heaven is no retirement village in the sky. It is where God's work is done more effectively because sin is gone. Where God is, there is work. It is a holy, everlasting calling and He loves it.

Business was central to new testament strategy!

If I were to ask you who were the key figures in the book of Acts in the spread of the gospel, following the outpouring of the Holy Spirit, who would you suggest? Peter? Paul?

What if I were to say that the five key figures included a value-added service provider, two people in manufacturing, one in the armed forces and a high-end fashion dealer?

Far fetched? Not really. Peter was working from the premises of Simon the Tanner – a value-added retailer. That's where he got his vision; that was his base for taking the gospel for the first time ever to the Gentiles. This incident included the armed forces in the guise of a Roman soldier, a strategic element, not only in spreading the gospel first to the Gentiles, but also through the Roman empire to Europe and beyond.

The two people in manufacturing were Priscilla and Aquilla, tent manufacturers. Paul met them in Athens and they worked together. The Church at Corinth was born out of the teamwork that ensued. Their manufacturing base was also the base from which Paul and the team operated. They travelled with Paul and the team. Paul leaves them at Ephesus. They risked their lives for him. All the churches of the Gentiles were recorded as being grateful for them. The Church – presumably in Corinth – met in their home. It was this husband and wife business team that straightened out Apollo's theology and gave him understanding. Paul called them his fellow-workers.

The high-end fashion designer was Lydia. A dealer in purple dye – high-end stuff. She was the first European convert and her network almost certainly sparked the first church in Europe. She provided a home for Paul and his team. The *first base for the first outreach team into Europe!*

Islam respects its business people for this very reason. Ask any informed person why Islam has a hold all over Africa and they will quickly point you to the shopkeepers, the traders and the merchantmen who carry their gospel, as they shamelessly and effectively live out their beliefs in a business setting. Every Moslem-dominated nation is rich in Islam-practising businessmen.

And most of them live out a prophetic lifestyle into the community. Only twice have I ever been taken to task over the quality of my Christianity and in both cases it was by Moslem businessmen.

It's also very effective at making its presence felt every morning, and again in the evening, in Kampala, Uganda. As with many hundreds of other African cities, there are very loud calls from the mosque for prayers, and there is no hesitation, wherever they are, the businessmen and women included will bow down and pray. Making their mark – a Moslem mark – on the surrounding people. How will Jesus be made known, and how will the glory of God be spread around your area? Almost certainly it will start where you work.

God works

God works! The very first verse in the Bible says, *'In the beginning God created (worked at) the heavens and the earth.'*

Then Genesis 2:3, *'Then God blessed the seventh day and sanctified it, because in it He rested from all His work which God had created and made.'*

In Genesis, describing the creation, God is recorded as one who *'makes, forms, builds and plants'*. These are all words used elsewhere in scripture to describe work.

Whilst God's work can be distinguished from our own by the fact that He is all-powerful and His work is perfect, His work did involve many of the functions we consider work to be:

* He makes things – as a craftsman might
* He categorises and names things – as a scientist might
* He plans carefully – one process following another
* He examines the quality of his work – quality control
* He clearly defines each component's function – as an engineer might
* He clearly defines humanity's role and provides resources – as a good manager might
* His work reflects who He is – as we would like ours to do
* He takes pleasure in his work – a job well done – satisfied

Right through the Bible, God is represented as constantly *working* – ordering circumstances to change our lives, getting involved in nations and in individuals. God is at *work* – ruling, delegating and providing. In Philippians 2:13, it says, *'for it is God who works in you both to will and to do for His good pleasure.'* Both His will and His **work** are His good pleasure.

Notice too that there is absolutely no distinction between the natural and the spiritual, God creating or working by His Spirit (see Genesis 1:2 – *'the Spirit of God was hovering over the face of the waters.'*) It also says clearly that God rested from His work . . .

Chapter 5

PRISON OR DESTINY?
THE BIG LIE

The big lie

The big lie has put many of God's people to sleep – like Sleeping Beauty, who pricked her finger, got poisoned and ended up sleeping longer than usual! She looks beautiful, is still breathing, but is basically ineffective and neutered. As a church, the sleeping drug still has traces in our bloodstream in the form of a big lie or heresy.

The heresy suggests that work is worldly or secular and that church activity or function is somehow spiritual or sacred. You won't find the words 'sacred' and 'secular' ever together in scripture. There is no such distinction and there is no such concept biblically. In fact the word secular does not appear in the Bible at all – not once!

From the very first chapter in the Bible, we get the clearest indication that true spiritual activity and work are synonymous. As we saw in Genesis 1:2 ('the Spirit of God was hovering over the face of the waters'), God was working, and working by the Holy Spirit. You can't get more spiritual than the Holy Spirit and the Holy Spirit works.

In Exodus chapter 35, we see one of the first records of God choosing men and putting His Holy Spirit on them. What for? To act as priests or congregational leaders? No! In verses 31–35, talking about a man named Bezalel, it says:

He has filled him with the Spirit of God, in wisdom and understanding, in knowledge and all manner of workmanship, to design artistic works, to work in gold and silver and bronze, in cutting jewels for setting, in carving wood, and to work in all manner of artistic workmanship. And He has put in his heart the ability to teach, in him and Aholiab the son of Ahisamach, of the tribe of Dan. He has filled them with skill to do all manner of work of the engraver and the designer and the tapestry maker, in blue, purple, and scarlet thread, and fine linen, and of the weaver – those who do every work and those who design artistic works.

They were filled by the Holy Spirit for excellence in various **work-based skills.**

Work was the first responsibility given to man. Before God gave Adam his wife and family, he gave him work. The Lord took the man and put him into the garden to *work* it and to take care of it. Adam was never placed on the planet to worship. He was placed here to work.

Eve was created and presented, because no helper was found, as Adam began the process of work. Work is not the result of the fall. Work was there before the fall, part of God's personality and integral to His faultless design. Work was to be part of Adam's richest fellowship with his Maker. The fall tainted work, and brought thorns to the rose bush and weeds to the flower displays. But the rose and the flower bed were there before and are still there now. Men and women together from the very beginning were created to have fellowship with each other, and with God, by working on His planet, serving each other and serving God in the process.

The thought of work evokes poetry from the very heart of God. In Psalm 104, the psalmist is describing the wonders of creation in poetry set to music. One of these wonders of creation is expressed in verse 23, where it says, 'Man goes out to his work and to his labour until the evening.' The psalmist goes on to sing out, in verse 31, 'May the glory of the Lord endure forever; may the Lord rejoice in His works', referring, along with several other dimensions of creation, to man going out to his *work*.

There is glory in our work. God made us in His image so that we can fulfil His purpose in ourselves and in the world by working.

Willliam Tyndale put it like this, 'There is no work better than another to please God; to pour water, to wash dishes, to be a cobbler, or an apostle, all is one; to wash dishes or to preach is all one as touching the deed, to please God.' When I was working with YWAM, Corrie Ten-Boom came up to me once when I was washing dishes and simply said, 'Young man, I would far rather be doing what you are doing than what I do.' She had picked up my frustration with dishwashing instead of preaching, and she was inserting into my life a one sentence, theological foundation.

George Macdonald put it this way:

> If the soul of the believer be the temple of the Holy Spirit, then is not the place of that man's labour – his shop, his bank, his laboratory, his school, his factory – the temple of Jesus Christ where the spirit of man is at work? Mr Drew, your shop is the temple of your service where the Lord Christ ought to be throned. Your counter ought to be His altar, and everything laid on it with the intent of doing as you can for your neighbour, in the name of Christ Jesus.

I often wondered why it was so difficult to penetrate successful businessmen with the message of God's Kingdom. I came to the conclusion that work is so spiritual, so God-like that it nearly fills the spiritual vacuum in the lives of people who give themselves to it. For that reason it can easily deceive them into thinking that the vacuum is in fact filled. The negative outcome is simply further evidence that work is spiritual, deeply spiritual.

The concept that work is secular is a pagan Greek concept that has so permeated church thinking and practice. It has castrated men and women who otherwise would have been productive. It has prevented God's people from seeing all they could be and do.

My life is full of both church work and business consultancy. I train people, run seminars and provide strategic and marketing consultancy. I also travel the world preaching, trying to be prophetic and sometimes the two dimensions seem to pull each other apart. I remember thinking often that my life was like the letter 'Y'. I used to have a regular moan at God, varying the flavour of the particular moan! Sometimes I used to pray like this: 'Lord, can't you just let me be a preacher? I could be a great preacher – I could ask Bob Mumford to train me.' Two weeks later, after a particularly successful time in business, my prayer would go like this: 'Lord, can't you just let me focus on business? If I were more focused, I could employ more people, and make large sums of money for your Kingdom.' In fact I used to pray, 'Lord, I feel like the two ends of the letter Y. Can't you just let me come into one or other, so that I have one emphasis and one focus? Lord, could it please be one or the other?' In other words, like the single stem at the bottom of the letter Y.

I had only told one person other than Gill what I was thinking and praying. So imagine my surprise when a preacher called Dennis Peacocke came off the platform at an event our church was hosting and said this: 'You see a Y, but it is not so, it is a single rod.' In other words, my Greek thinking was separating the two compartments – church/business, secular/sacred, consultancy/ministry. God was saying as clearly as if He were in the room, 'It isn't like that, it is single life flow.' It has taken many years for that to permeate my mind and heart, but it was a foundational understanding. I had known that in theory, but this was God's word making it real to me.

So as long as this great lie, this powerful drug, has traces in our bloodstream, it will affect how we feel about ourselves, about the *value* of what we do, and give us a false perspective about the Church. Full-time or any form of work in the Church is not more spiritual. It is not more highly valued by God. The Church is not the Kingdom nor is work, but both have a vital part to play in its application. It is not 'either/or', it is 'both/and'.

If you and I are called to what we do, there is nothing more spiritual, nothing more wonderful. When we see that, the last traces of sleeping drug evaporate, a trumpet sounds in heaven, and a patiently waiting God – infinitely creative – can begin to lavishly dispense His Spirit, His wisdom, His counsel and His gifts, to a channel through which His power and purpose can be poured.

The enemy has taught God's people to view work as secular. I hear the term used often – it does us no service. The enemy has taught the Church to view work as less spiritual, second best to church activity. It's a lie; it's time to purge the drug from our system. The issue is not 'sacred or secular?' The issue is, 'Is what I do in the flesh or in the Spirit?' That question, by the way, is equally valid to those paid by the Church and those paid by their labours in a different sphere.

When we view work as secular it has profound implications. Why? Because it takes meaning, value and a sense of calling away from what we do. It will cripple faith. It will cause the will, the works and the power of God to evaporate.

In our church, if we have a membership of, say, 50, at best there may be 2 to 3 functions paid fully or partially by the church. What does that mean to the remaining 47? Are we somehow less spiritual, less useful and less valuable to God? I don't think so! The reason is found in our next heading . . .

Destiny for most of us will be outside the Church and in our place of work

It is important, in this context, to believe that destiny for most of us will not primarily be in the church gathering or the church context. For many of us this can cause enormous frustrations and tensions.

We can't see our ultimate destiny or calling in the Church and yet somehow we feel reluctant, guilty, carnal or even second best if we begin to consider options that extend beyond the Church's sphere or realm.

I have heard it said, directly and by implication, that really spiritual men – men who have 'made it' in God – will become 'full-time'. The belief system we have discussed, and some elements of our own church culture, have produced a generation of men and women who have a deep-seated conviction, or a deep longing and hope, that they will be ultimately called to this so called 'full-time' ministry.

Over the years I have spoken to hundreds, probably thousands, who feel this way and who deep down believe this is their end or destiny, or who desperately hope that it is.

This is subtle – subtle because it seems godly, or at least reasonable. In reality it is a robber. It robs our employer of a whole heart, of a whole commitment. It can rob us of our destiny. We can work legally and fulfil the obligations of our job but our heart will never be fully in what we are doing. It can rob gifted entrepreneurs from releasing their faith and releasing that gifting. It 'strokes' the darker side of our heart, that makes excuses when it can, to avoid risk, discomfort or danger. It produces in us a short term mentality towards work – deep down always hoping for, always longing for, the call to 'higher things'.

The choice of language is revealing. The Church is not a 'higher thing', the Church is not more spiritual, than the sphere in which we should be living out our destiny. Work, in whatever context, is the most spiritual thing you can ever do, providing God has called you to it.

Church was never meant to be the sum total of my walk with God – or even a high percentage of it. It is the family base from which I do my real work and to which I am accountable. Church can never be the full expression of my calling, it is the equipping centre to enable me to fulfil it. My destiny is not the Church; the Church is there to ensure that I fulfil my destiny wherever God has called me.

The Church is not to be a parasite, sucking into itself all the most able, most qualified, most spiritual. It needs to equip those individuals and fling them out into every sphere of service, work and activity. Look at Ephesians 4:12 – 'for the equipping of the saints for the work of ministry'. We don't hold all the best to ourselves – we are to give our best freely.

This fact then prompts another self-evident question. Are you called by God to your place of work? I am shocked by the fact that many godly people don't know, have never thought about it or don't care!!! I am even more shocked by the general absence of the Holy Spirit's anointing and power evidenced in our places of work.

One of the sobering facts to realise is that work occupies more than half of our waking hours. The other half is divided into family time (work on the house, garden, etc), church involvement, time alone with God and relaxation. So the sum of these things (family, relaxing, church, time with God) – *the sum of them* – is equal in time to the time spent working.

We will spend more time working than we will in any one of those other areas. It is, therefore, of extreme weight and importance – 40 to 50 hours a week working, as against say 8 to 10 hours in a direct church function, and maybe 20 hours doing other things at home.

If we are not certain that our job is the call of God on our lives, we run the risk of wasting the best part of each day, each week and each year. If we are not certain that our job is the call of God for now, it means that half of our life can easily and in reality be spent outside the will of God.

If I don't have this view of the calling of God to my work, then it has ceased to be a calling and become a pain, and money has become the compensation for it!! If that is what I think or feel, then I am living unbiblically and sooner or later it will take its toll. The most likely outcome is that money will become increasingly important and that is what I will work for. Money makes a lousy master and you can't serve God and mammon.

If work is really spiritual, if it is in reality the place of our calling and destiny, then with the call of God comes the anointing, the power and the workings of God in the changing of lives as they touch ours. If we don't believe that this is God's call, we will not expect anointing, we will not expect God's life to pulsate through us in our working environment, and sure enough we won't get it!

The effect of all this!

If we know that our work is the calling of God, we can reach out positively in faith for the anointing. If we see work as spiritual, as our prime place of function and destiny, then let us call on the Holy Spirit and believe that His power, His gifts and His anointing will fill us and work supernaturally through us. My question is, 'Where are the men and women of the Holy Spirit, who can impact the world of work in this way?'

In work, my daily motive should be that God has called me here. This is where I will interface or introduce the Kingdom of God. I work because I am called to it, and it's my primary sphere to live out what it means to 'seek first the Kingdom of God'.

It is time to settle the issue. Time is short and our lives are short. Why do I do what I do? Am I in it because it is easy? Am I in it because of the money it makes? Am I in it for myself, adding God to what I want to do? Or am I in it because I am confident it is where God has placed me for now? It is time to settle the fact that my work is not an accident, it is where God has called me and it is where He has placed me.

Housewife, student, factory worker, office worker, medical worker, entrepreneur. Are we doing whatever we are doing because we are disciples and this is where He has led us? If that is our primary motivation above all the others, then we will bring pleasure to God and release His power. If we have settled the issue, if we know we are called of God, if our motives are pure, then we can legitimately expect God to anoint us, expect Him to move and our faith and expectation levels can grow:

1. The power of the Holy Spirit is daily open to me.

2. I can be a witness, and in that process see people touched and born again.

3. Spiritual gifts can be used in the working environment (Jesus' use of the gifts was something like 70% in the non-church environment – in the streets, whilst travelling, on outward-bound courses, with business people, with local leaders, under trees, etc.)

4. I can be alert to pre-ordained people contacts.

5. I can begin the journey of learning what it really means to see the Kingdom of God become a reality in my sphere of responsibility.

I want to encourage us to find a place of faith – faith for our jobs and our businesses, faith for the projects we are responsible for. I want to encourage us to see work as a high calling, to see it as valid and as valuable.

I want us to have the peace and joy that come with knowing that we are in the centre of God's will – not just as a stop-gap. I want to urge us, require of us, that we find faith in our work – daily faith, long term faith. We have heard it said so many times that without faith it is impossible to please God. Whatever does not proceed from faith is sin. Can we find it? Can we feel the fresh wind of God blowing hope, anticipation and faith once more?

. . . Faith to believe that God wants this current outpouring to flow through our farms, our offices, our homes, our colleges and universities, our factories, our practices, our consultancies.

. . . Faith to believe that God can, and in fact has planned to, use me in the process.

. . . Faith to believe that I am where He has called me.

In short, faith to believe and practice work as place of function and not a prison. Destiny – a high calling – a joy to ourselves and a pleasure to the heart of God!

Chapter 6

SIX MONTHS WITHOUT PAY!

A friend of mine in British Columbia, Canada, told a powerful story, which impacted me with some strength and has haunted me in a way ever since. He was working as a director of a small exhibition centre. At one point, the federal government cut off all funding to the programme, which meant that all the directors were laid off.

My friend had taught that 'we work for God and not for pay', and felt that this moment was a test of his own conviction. Having shared with some wise leaders and his own dad, he carried on his job without any guaranteed pay. One day he decided to knock off early. As he was turning the key in the door, he sensed God saying, 'Why are you leaving early?' His response was, 'But I'm not getting paid!' to which he sensed God saying, 'That depends on who your employer is.' Needless to say, he went back to work – and did just that for over six months. During this time God provided for the family's needs in a variety of ways.

Just over six months into the experience, the federal government reviewed its funding of the exhibition centres. Out of three centres located in Western Canada, his centre was chosen for funding. As part of their package they voluntarily reimbursed him with full back pay. That back pay enabled him to pay off his mortgage in full!

What a great story! Really? I find it an uncomfortable challenge going right to the heart, to the root motives, to the reason why I work. In this context there are a lot of religious thoughts and ideas around the motive for working.

In the issue of motives and motivation, what is pure and what is impure? It is important to be able to distinguish between 'fruit' and 'root'. Confusion between the two can lead to disillusionment and Divine resistance.

What does the Bible say?

If I asked you now to tell me why you work and to give me a Biblical basis for your answer, I wonder what you would say? I wonder, too, if that would be your real belief. What does the Bible say? Let's look at just a handful of scriptures:

Matthew 6:33: 'But seek first the kingdom of God and His righteousness, and all these things shall be added to you.'

2 Thess 3:10–15: 'For even when we were with you, we commanded you this: If anyone will not work, neither shall he eat. For we hear that there are some who walk among you in a disorderly manner, not working at all, but are busybodies. Now those who are such we command and exhort through our Lord Jesus Christ that they work in quietness and eat their own bread. But as for you, brethren, do not grow weary in doing good. And if anyone does not obey our word in this epistle, note that person and do not keep company with him, that he may be ashamed. Yet do not count him as an enemy, but admonish him as a brother.'

1 Thess 4:11–12: 'Aspire to lead a quiet life, to mind your own business, and to work with your own hands, as we commanded you, that you may walk properly toward those who are outside, and that you may lack nothing.'

Col 3:22–25 and 4:1,2: 'Bondservants, obey in all things your masters according to the flesh, not with eyeservice, as men-pleasers, but in sincerity of heart, fearing God. And whatever you do, do it heartily, as to the Lord and not to men, knowing that from the Lord you will receive the reward of the inheritance; for you serve the Lord Christ. But he who does wrong will be repaid for what he has done, and there is no partiality. Masters, give your bondservants what is just and fair, knowing that you also have a Master in heaven. Continue earnestly in prayer, being vigilant in it with thanksgiving.'

Eccles 8:15: 'So I commended enjoyment, because a man has nothing better under the sun than to eat, drink, and be merry; for this will remain with him in his labour all the days of his life which God gives him under the sun.'

Eccles 3:22: 'So I perceived that nothing is better than that a man should rejoice in his own works, for that is his heritage. For who can bring him to see what will happen after him?'

Eccles 2:24–26: 'Nothing is better for a man than that he should eat and drink, and that his soul should enjoy good in his labour. This also, I saw, was from the hand of God. For who can eat, or who can have enjoyment, more than I? For God gives wisdom and knowledge and joy to a man who is good in His sight; but to the sinner He gives the work of gathering and collecting, that he may give to him who is good before God. This also is vanity and grasping for the wind.'

Prov 22:29: 'Do you see a man who excels in his work? He will stand before kings; he will not stand before unknown men.'

A pure root

We have begun to see a vision; what kind of people will it take to fulfil that vision? What kind of attitudes and motives are required? From these scriptures, as well as others we have already looked at, we can deduce some pure reasons for work and some pure motives.

1. *'Seek first the Kingdom . . .'* In these words, Jesus expressed the true motive – seek first the Kingdom of God, and all these things will be added to you. Notice the key word – *added* – not taken. The real difference between prosperity and covetousness is that prosperity is given whilst covetousness wants to take it, and take it now. All things may indeed be *added,* but a pure root is, 'I work where I do because I am called, led, directed by a working God, and it is my primary sphere, where I work out what it means to seek first the Kingdom of God.'

2. I work because it is a fundamental instruction – *'If anyone will not work, neither shall he eat . . . if anyone does not obey our word in this epistle . . . work with your own hands, as we commanded you . . .'* In other words, I should be so crystal clear, there should be no doubt that this is my minimum contribution to life on this earth. It is what I was created to do, and if I don't do it I shouldn't live. That is pretty strong, isn't it, but it is for my own good, because . . .

3. *'. . . a man should rejoice in his own works.'* I work because it is good for me. God has given it to me to enjoy. When I work there is something of the self-fulfilling joy of God that courses through my life. It gives meaning, it gives pleasure and it gives a wholesome outlet to express what God Himself has placed within me. When I work, because God Himself works, I touch in some mysterious way the Trinity itself.

4. I do it for Jesus, not for money, not for the Church, not for anything other than God himself. *'And whatever you do, do it heartily, as to the Lord and not to men, knowing that from the Lord you will receive the reward of the inheritance; for you serve the Lord Christ.'* What a liberating concept! Even in the worst of all working conditions – slavery – Paul says, 'You are doing it for Jesus, so do it with your whole heart – it is him you are serving.' I can't tell you the hundreds of times I have counselled men and women who tell me, 'We are desperate to serve Jesus but simply don't know what his will is.' Friend, the will of God is in front of your hands and noses, go and do some work and work at it with all your heart and might. Do it for Him and for no other primary reason, and be sure there is an inheritance of eternal significance for you. But beyond that, just try it with a glad heart and see ever-increasing horizons open up for you as the Kingdom of God unfolds in your life.

You can spend the whole of your life waiting to hear from God about how you can serve Him, and miss it right in your own back yard. Pastors and leaders, encourage your folks to work with all their hearts where they are, and watch the leaven of the Kingdom get kick-started in your church. Watch the Church grow around you, as you fearlessly encourage your people to do what they were put on this planet to do.

If we will get this lot in our motivational bloodstream, we might just find ourselves able to work six months without pay! Without these four pillars we certainly will not.

Common errors

Some common errors in motives I have heard over the years include the following:

Error 1 – to provide for my family

This confuses some people. What about the scripture in 1Tim 5:8, which says, *'But if anyone does not provide for his own, and especially for those of his household, he has denied the faith and is worse than an unbeliever'*? If we don't work, we should not eat! Sure, but that is the most extreme basic laid down for lazy people – it is not the 'raison d'être' for positive God-inspired work. Similarly, provision for my family is not the primary reason for working. If it is in reality, then it forms the root of the tree and the tree will be stunted and deformed. The root should be that I am created for this, this is what He has placed me here to do and I am called by God to do it joyfully and whole-heartedly. The tree with roots like that will be beautiful, and the fruit it bears will provide for and prepare me. The inevitable downside of a motivation like this is limited commitment to my job, limited faith, limited creativity and limited energy.

Error 2 – to support me so that I can do the important bit in the Church!!

This is sickeningly insidious. It has religiosity right the way through it, but it is a sticky, slimy error. What does it produce? – a short term mentality. I will never truly see or apprehend why God has placed me where I am. I will always be looking for the higher thing. This is dangerous – it sounds so pure and so holy, but it is a leprous growth upon our souls, which eats away the life almost imperceptibly and without feeling, but the odour and the sight of it plague many hundreds of men and women I have spoken to over the years. A person with this drive will ultimately lose the respect of his colleagues. He or she will not be highly employable, because their heart will not be fully in the job. And ultimately it will surely lead to disillu-sionment.

Error 3 – to bring financial prosperity

This is a well-taught heresy in some movements and we will look at it in detail in chapter twelve. We don't work to prosper, that is not what drives us nor is it our primary aim. That doesn't mean I don't believe in profit, in fact I believe irresponsible losses are a sin. But as a motive, as a drive, it is a rights-orien-tated, manipulative approach to God. It hides a whole can of hidden soul worms; it is a mirror right into the deepest decep-tions of my heart and what it shows me is not terribly pleasant. The most common outcome I have seen, so far, is that a love for money gets an insatiable hold of many men and women working for prosperity.

Error 4 – status or career advancement

I do believe with all my heart in career advancement. I believe in Joseph, Daniel and Esther rising to the top of their environments. I believe in commitment and excellence providing a basis for that to happen. But that is not to be our drive, or our motivation, for self-serving reasons. I believe in men and women at the top of every sphere of society serving God there. But that is the focus – *serving God there* – not status there, or career advancement there. The line between the two approaches may be a fine one, but it is surely there. And the heart knows, better than we do, how to hide that difference. If this is our motivation, then sooner or later selfishness will accelerate and pride will produce the normal crop of spiritual barrenness and dryness. The loss of life and the imperceptible growth in arrogance will leave our friends mourning the loss of a once God-serving man or woman. As a 'raison d'être' it's deficient, because self rather than God is the focus.

Error 5 – to provide for the Church

Again this can be so wonderfully camouflaged. I know the scriptures about generous giving and about storing treasure in heaven, but I do not work to provide for the Church. What arrogance! Is the Church dependant on me or upon God? If the answer, dear church leader, is me, then what we are producing is not the true church but a cult. I will preach responsibility in finance with the rest and I believe in giving every bit as much as the rest, but as a reason for work it is another concealed deception. I have seen churches dependent on one or two wealthy individuals for finance. That is danger time. I have actually counselled numbers who wanted to start a business to provide for the Church. Every one I know about personally has gone to the wall. I suspect God will see to it that it will go to the wall! I even had one man eating at our family dining table, who said, 'I tithe to the Church from the business, so God is obligated to ensure I prosper – He must do it.' That business lasted just a few more months. This motive often hides a secret love for money camouflaged by religious hypocrisy.

Each one of these five may well be a *fruit* of getting it right, but should never be the *root*, the reason why we do a particular job or start a particular business.

Incorrect attitudes at work

We have talked about errors in thinking, but what about incorrect attitudes?

1. A deep-seated conviction that I am ultimately called to full-time ministry and this is only a temporary stop-gap whilst I wait for and train for higher things. The concept of 'higher things' is a heresy and needs nailing. The practical outworking of this conviction is a robbery. I will rob my business, my employer, my work colleagues of my full attention and energy. I will always be longing for that higher stage in my life and I will miss the present. I remember one manager at a company called Technicon who said to me, 'David, I need more staff but I don't want Christians because their commitment is not really wholehearted.' He wasn't talking about a company that wanted men and women to sell their souls. He was talking about a lack of wholeheartedness for this very reason. I am happy to say that over a period of a year or so we gave him some of the highest results he had ever had. Lack of wholeheartedness is a barrier. In 2 Chronicles it says, 'He sought the Lord and worked wholeheartedly and so he prospered.' And in James, 'for he who doubts is like a wave of the sea driven and tossed by the wind. For let not that man suppose that he will receive anything from the Lord.'

2. We are not certain that our job is the call of God for now on our lives. That means that half of our lives, or more, can in reality be lived outside the will of God. With the call of God comes the anointing, the power, the working of God in changing of lives as they touch ours. If we don't believe this is the call of God, then we won't expect God's life to pulsate through us in our working environment and sure enough we will not get it.

3. I am working to get not give. There is often a welfare mentality in our approach to work. That's why, for many, the thought of working without pay is very alien. If we are truly working for Jesus with a whole heart, then we will truly be working to give and not just to get. In my attitudes to reward, two key attitudes should prevail – gratitude and contentment. The world's mould and pressure is a constant barrage of ingratitude, discontentment and demands. Materialism is wanting things *now* – that new kitchen, suite, clothes – now! God's way is to add these things – but on His timescale. If we lose gratitude it is easy to allow a root of bitterness to spring up and defile.

If we can settle the issues in this chapter, some wonderful possibilities flow from our work. We will discover that work is not solely for our own needs and satisfaction. We will discover that work enables us to give to those less fortunate than ourselves.

4. If I am unemployed, it is not right for me to work when I am on state benefit. I have heard this a few times over the years. If you are unemployed, may God bless you and encourage you – it's a horrible place to be. But if you want to get a job, do some work without pay! I have interviewed scores of job applicants over the years. Many of them have been unemployed and most of those were unemployable. Why? Because they were not working. If I am looking to employ someone for a job, I want a hardworking person who does not need nagging, who is motivated to work and who enjoys work. If you are unemployed and not working, you don't fit that category by definition. This is not hard or judgmental, this is common sense advice from an employer wanting to help you find a job! One of the few warnings in the New Testament is 'warn those who are idle.' Take it from me, idle people surface early on in a job interview and an employer would be unwise in the extreme to offer a job – 'He who hires a fool or a passer-by wounds everyone.'

The raison d'être for work

Work is not there to provide a big tithe for the Church.

Work is not there to provide God with money that he is otherwise short of.

Work is not there to be 'tent making', to enable me to fulfil my *ministry*.

Work is not there for our prosperity.

Work is not there for our personal fulfilment.

Work is not there to train us for leadership.

Work may indeed provide some of these elements, but they are fruits, they are not the root or the raison d'être. The raison d'être is simply that God works and we are created in his image to do likewise. For most of us, we will express the destiny, the high calling of God primarily through work. If we will believe that – if faith will rise to that – then the dynamic of God's kingdom, the Holy Spirit, will be available, with infinite power and infinite creativity to make his impression through us, an impression of God's Kingdom in our sphere of work.

Work enables us to serve others and thereby contribute to community life. God is a Holy Trinity of sacrificial love, total openness, complete trust. I heard it said in one of the Spring Harvest seminars – 'Other people do not threaten me, they complete me. I become truly free when I open my life for others and share it with them, and when others respond likewise. Then the other person is no longer a limitation on my freedom but the completion of it.'

Work enables us to develop gifts and skills and express ourselves.

An anonymous Jewish millionaire said, 'work exists to fulfil human needs and social responsibilities.'

It is not *what* we do that determines value, but whom we do it for. It is not *how well* we do it, but in whose strength.

A check list!

Read through the following statements and tick the three which most accurately reflect what you really believe are your motives for working:

☐ I work primarily to provide for myself and my family.

☐ I work to earn enough to enable me to do my real work for God.

☐ I work to support others in the church.

☐ I work as a means to financial prosperity.

☐ I am working as a stop-gap until I sense God's calling on my life.

☐ I work because I have been created to do just that, and it is where I practically outwork 'seeking first the Kingdom of God'.

Thanks for doing that. Now rank those three in order of real importance to you (1, 2, 3). How do your three choices line up with this chapter and what changes could you make?

Almost certainly, the anvil will be the place where those changes are implemented or effected in you!

Chapter 7

GOD'S ANVIL

I love to watch the blacksmith. There is something carrying eternal touches when you see fire and pressure applied to unyielding, dirty-looking, raw iron. One thing is for sure, without that heat and the smashing process, that raw material is simply not going to change. Hammer it without heat and all you will do is dent it. Heat it without the hammer and all you have is hot potential. In Isaiah, God says, 'I **created** you, O Jacob, I **formed** you, O Israel.' The Hebrew for **create** means producing out of nothing. The Hebrew for **forming** carries with it the idea of a process, which changes shapes and moulds us. He could make Jacob out of nothing, but Israel was formed through divinely ordered processes. The 'supplanter' was created, the 'one who struggles with God and overcomes' was formed.

When a Samurai sword is made, it is heated, hammered over and cooled down. Heated, hammered over, cooled down. It is that harsh repetitive process that gives it its unique strength and its ultimate sharpness. There is no other way to do it. James 1:5 puts it like this: 'If any of you lacks wisdom, let him ask of God, who gives to all liberally and without reproach, and it will be given to him.' What does he give liberally? Look at verse 2 and you will find the answer – 'all kinds of trials'. Loads of them! Do you still want wisdom? The passage goes on to say, in verse 3, 'knowing that the testing of your faith produces patience.' Patience, or perseverance, must finish its work so that you may be complete or mature, not lacking anything.

The word *testing* is a word for proving and refers to the crucible. In Malachi, it talks about God's refiner's fire. In the Old Testament times, they would suspend gold in a crucible or melting pot over the hottest fire the refiner could produce. As the metal seethed in the pot, the 'dross' or impurities would force their way to the surface and be skimmed off. The process was repeated until all the impurities were removed. The refiner was not satisfied until he could see his own face clearly in the metal. Metals that passed the test of refining were accepted, metals that failed the test were rejected.

Does this ring any bells? It certainly does in my life! The anvil of work has the ability to cross my will like little else.

The Father's anvil for His Son

Jesus knew this crucible. Jesus knew this anvil process. It says of him that 'He learnt obedience through the things he suffered.' That's a nice verse. I have heard it preached many times in a vague way. But come on now, how does this work in practice? This is not semantics. The Son of God was called the 'Son of Man' for good reason. He bled when cut, He was 'tempted in all points like we are yet without sin.' He faced forty days and nights in the wilderness where He was tempted. But it tells us, as clear as a bell, that He learned obedience through the things He suffered. What does that mean? Well, it surely includes the years from twelve to thirty where he was working as 'the carpenter'. His ability to hear God was already budding at twelve. We can see that for ourselves in the Temple. But where did He learn to hear his Father with increasing clarity? Where did He develop the strength of character for His forty day fast and ultimate face-to-face with Satan?

Where did the strength of resolve to handle the garden of Gethsemane come from? ('If it is possible, let this cup pass from me; nevertheless, not as I will, but as You will.') How could He handle sweating great drops of blood and still not reach out for the twelve legions of angels? Because, in eighteen years, He had learned in the anvil of work. The world of work was the Father's anvil for the Son that He loved, the Son who pleased Him, the perfect Son.

I have seen this in a small way with my own children. We have done lots of memorable things together. We pioneered, with an organisation called High Force, 'Father & Son' and 'Father & Daughter' events to provide marvellous, unforgettable experiences together. But the most memorable, the most life changing events, have often come through the world of work. I remember some months back videoing Joshua's last day on his paper round and sending a copy to his brother Joel. Why? Because that was Joshua's first job, which had been passed on to him by his brother. They had both spent three years learning obedience through the weather they suffered, the extra houses they delivered to and commitment when ill. I was proud of their achievement and content, for a moment at least, with what they had learned.

When we moved into our current home, the landscape gardener offered to pay Joel to move some huge rocks, from the bottom of a very steep bank, up to the garden itself. Joel came up to my office after twenty minutes, dispirited and lonely. 'No way am I going to move all that on my own!' he said. I said nothing. He came back a few minutes later. 'Set your clock', he said. 'I am going to do it in two hours, and I am going to do it for you.' Sure enough, it was done. At thirteen, Joel had learned one of the most powerful lessons imaginable about money, motivation and relationships at work. Where else would he learn that?

Work is a marvellous mirror of reality. At work you can't rationalise or spiritualise failure or mistakes. You can't say, 'I'm sure my decision was the will of God', when you just lost your employer £50,000 in a negotiation. Market research shows that the average employer is not over impressed with Romans 8:28 – he prefers to call a failure a failure!

So for this reason and many others, work, in truth, is God's main tool to shape us into what we should be. That is not to say that character development is the raison d'être for work; it is however one of its fruits. Two specific areas spring to mind –

1. Wisdom

If our motives are right, wisdom will automatically and increasingly be added to who we are. Jesus said that the sons of this age learn wisdom from the real world of work and don't spend hours spiritualising.

If we embrace the mistakes, the admonishments, the correction and the successes in our God-filtered, God-ordered working environment, then we will become wiser. Again we tend to think of wisdom as related to the spiritual realm – church, Bible, meetings. Actually, the fear of the Lord begins right where we are. Proverbs tells us that 'wisdom cries out in streets and in city gateways' – the place of commerce.

2. Ruling

A lot has been theorised, in some churches, about ruling or discipling the nations. The one environment above others, where we will find a chance of learning that skill, is the eight-plus hours a day, 220 days a year spent at work.

Many of us will have been taught that the Kingdom of God involves us ruling, or taking responsibility for, the sphere in which God has placed us. Along with the family, work is a prime area to learn how to rule yourself, how to rule in the sphere where God places you and, where appropriate, how to rule others. The fall of Satan has continually sought to bring destruction to work – to bring selfishness, misery, poverty, repression, lack of discipline, lack of government and all kinds of fears and resentments. We can bring redemption to that sphere which God gives us. We can open the door for the Kingdom of God to impact that area. We can be the head and not the tail.

Joseph ultimately ruled a nation very successfully and this had much to do with his skill development through work. Think of his path – from dream to pit, to Potiphar, to prison, to Prime Minister. Where did he learn to hone his dream-interpreting? Where did he learn his administrative skills, which, by the way, also saved the nation of Israel? On the anvil of work.

Daniel, as a teenager, became a prisoner of war. Taken hundreds of miles away, forced to have a name change and positioned in such a way that he would never see his family again. Through the years, Daniel not only survived the Babylonian rule, but eventually came to govern a third of the kingdom. He was known as a man with extraordinary spirit. He had angelic encounters, miraculous experiences with wild beasts and supernatural equipping in the realm of dreams and revelation. Where did he exercise these attributes? Where did he learn to become a man of extraordinary spirit? On the anvil of work.

One of the great areas of ruling is patience. This tests me to the hilt, and never more than when Joel came home after two years away and set up his office close to mine. I have preached the 'father & son' model for years and longed for the day when one of my kids would put it into practice. I was busy revising my theology after the first day! Joel likes to interrupt – I mean not just once a day, but let's say once or twice every thirty minutes. That, dear mathematical reader, is four times each hour – a staggering thirty-two interruptions per day!

After the first few days I was getting vexed and it showed, because there was a very quiet appearance at my office door and when I looked up there was no-one there. However, stuck to my door with BluTack, was the following quotation: 'Interruptions can be viewed as sources of irritation or opportunities for service, as moments lost or experience gained, as time wasted or horizons widened. They can annoy us or enrich us, get under our skin or give us a shot in the arm, monopolise our minutes or spice our schedules, depending on our attitude toward them.'

I had been got!! But that's the nature of the anvil.

Reputation

The Timothy and Titus qualifications for elders and deacons are based on *character* rather than *ministry*. In fact, if you count them – I did once – you will find thirty-three character-related and just one ministry-related statements. Where are we going to find a reputation like that, particularly with outsiders?

We know that ministry flows out of what we are. We can never minister what we are not, or what we don't have. We can *act* it. But we cannot *minister* it. Leadership in the Body should be a reflection of what you are at work. Work is not there to pay for you to be a leader. Work is not there to make you a leader. Work, as we have said, is there as God's calling for our life, the fruit of which will be a man or woman who can be called and anointed of God to minister in the Church. Many great men and women of God have learned how to rule, lead or govern through the world of work.

Faith

The place of work, for so many obvious reasons, is the place of faith development. I have clients who call me from time-to-time to ask me to pray for their sales this month. I had a client e-mail me this morning and ask me to pray for one of his assignments, because an advert had unexpectedly bombed and he was at a loss what to do. Why would they do that? Because they understand that a seamless God is interested in the month's sales figures, is interested in anxiety over work done that has not yet been successful.

Most of the business ventures I have undertaken have been steps, sometimes leaps, of faith. What does that mean in practice? It means, in reality, that I didn't have all the resources or skills necessary for the successful implementation of the project. It means that I approached it with apprehension. It also means that I believed I had heard God and my confidence would be in that word.

Everyone who is growing in faith will frequently be pushed or pulled into circumstances where more faith is needed. And, by its very nature, faith insists that I operate beyond the realms of the known into the unknown.

Have you noticed the biblical emphasis, *live* by faith. Normal Christian life will regularly and increasingly become full of faith. Faith for every day – faith for every area. Faith, faith, faith. Faith is not occasional, not just for significant critical moments in life, but daily life. If we are not increasingly living by faith, then something is wrong.

Living by faith does not mean, in biblical terms, that you are a church-paid worker. The truth is some church-paid Christian workers talk about living by faith when they mean their salary is paid by the Church, and in fact they may exercise very little real faith at all. Faith is for every Christian in every sphere of life, for every day, for every part of our life. To live as a Christian can only be real, meaningful dynamite when we live by faith, as we learn to bring every area of our life under the Lordship of Jesus. So we need to bring every area of our life under faith. In Romans, we learn that the businessman Abraham is 'the father of all those who **walk** in the **footsteps** of the faith.' Galatians says, 'Since we live by the Spirit let us keep in step with the Spirit' (or 'let us walk with the Spirit'). God is so practical, so helpful – here He brings living in faith down to manageable steps, literally footsteps. Faith and the Spirit are inseparable – to walk in the footsteps of the faith is the same as walking in the footsteps of the Holy Spirit. Keeping in step with the Spirit is the same as walking, or keeping in step, with faith.

What does this mean in practice? Simply that, like many other great truths, we apply them in daily chunks – learning what it means to walk in faith. Taking one step after another it's easy, it's manageable, it's possible, it's for you and me. We hear God and do it in faith. We can apply this to software bugs, to difficult patients, to late payment, to business development, to shop floor difficulties and to problem relationships – faith.

Without faith it is impossible to please God. Whatever does not proceed from faith is sin. What a fantastic opportunity to rise up to God's norm for our world of work! Faith is the believing into visibility of invisible realities. Where better than work to live that, grow into that, let that spill over into every area of our lives?

Faith outside of God is not biblical faith. Faith in men (other leaders, prophecies alone, church, family) is not biblical faith.

Why? Because all these things are fallible and God is not. Every leader you ever work with will fail in some way or other, and often God will allow hurt in those relationships. Why? Because He wants, and needs, to be sure that your faith is in Him and His Word and not in men or organisations. Faith begins by hearing, and in particular hearing the Word of God. It produces a response of faith in our heart. We speak it out with our mouth and we receive. Faith is never far away, it is always near us – namely in our mouth and in our heart. It does not require fantastic deeds or vision – ascending into heaven or descending into the deep. When we reach out for faith, God is not far away, not locked in heaven, not locked in the deep, but God's power is there in our hearts and mouths waiting to be received.

Work is likely to be the place where we will need to hear God the most and where in reality, if we are tuned in, if we are properly founded, if we are genuinely motivated, we can expect to hear God the most.

God's Anvil – **where character is hammered out**, where destiny is unlocked, where faith is released and where our seamless ministry comes into its fullness.

Chapter 8

WATCH OUT FOR THE WOLF

You may be forgiven for thinking, so far, that this guy has really got it in for the Church. You may have cried, 'Amen!' when I have had the occasional dig at church doctrine and church practice or even church leaders. Let's see how far the *Amens* go now! I can say what I say, because in my heart there is a settled issue regarding the Church. I can say what I say about leaders, because I am one and pleased to be.

The last fifteen years have been a journey for many of us as we have sought to 'seek first the Kingdom of God'. For me, at least, there have been imbalances in emphasis, there have been painful mistakes, there have also been great joys and exciting discoveries. In this chapter, with God's help, I hope to nudge the swinging pendulum back slightly. I'm aware that what I'm going to say is a pointer more than a conclusion. For some it may present a challenge, for others it may simply help to define what the Spirit of God is already stirring in you.

The Church is no accident for people at work

Ephesus was the most important town in Asia Minor, now Turkey. It had a harbour that opened into a river called the Caystem River, which in turn emptied into the Aegean Sea. It had few equals anywhere in the world. Certainly no city in Asia was more famous or more populous – it ranked with Rome, Corinth, Antioch, and Alexandria as one of the main urban centres of the empire. The city boasted impressive monuments including the temple of Diana (Artemis), one of the seven wonders of the world. Coins of the city were stamped with 'Neokoros' – temple warden.

It is into this modern, successful, cultural, political and economic environment that Paul writes with power about God's plan for the Church, God's view of the Church, and the Church's role. In Matthew's Gospel, Jesus gives a name to His plan for our world – and that name was 'Church'.

What does the name 'Church' mean? Most of you know this well. In the Greek, the word is Ekklesia ('Ek' means 'out of'; 'Klesis' means 'a calling'). It was used in ordinary Greek language to describe a group of citizens who were gathered to discuss the affairs of state. But when the word is used in Matthew, and then throughout the New Testament, it is invested by God with a much more significant and precise meaning. A meaning that affects hell and the powers of darkness. A meaning that gives every Christian an identity, an environment and a definition.

It is never used to describe a building. It is not meant to describe a meeting – we don't *go to* church, we *are* the Church. It is not meant to describe a denomination, group or stream. The Methodist church in Basingstoke is not the Church, it is simply a part of the Church in Basingstoke. When we are born again and become a Christian, we are added to the Church and we are 'called out' – called out of darkness, called out of being self-sufficient and called into His Church – a new world, a new environment with wonderful promises, protection, provision and responsibilities. Whether we like it or not, whether we know it or not, when we're born again we're in God's Church and nothing is going to change that. It's God's name for what we are now a part of.

There are 109 references to church in the New Testament. The New Testament is, in the main, a collection of letters written to churches in particular and the whole Church in general. Seven times in Revelation, we are told, 'he who has an ear, let him hear what the Spirit says to the churches.'

So the Church is no accident – it is God's choice of word, God's choice of structure and God's choice for us, the called-out ones, that very definitely includes you and me in our place of work.

The Church is strategic

The first time the word is used in the New Testament, it is in the context of the powers of darkness – 'I will build my **church** and the gates of Hades will not overcome it.' Hades was the Greek word for the place of departed spirits. The phrase here probably means powers of death or all forces opposed to Christ and His Kingdom. Satan's ultimate is death. Even that ultimate expression of Satan's activity will not overcome the Church.

This then is picked up strongly in Ephesians 3:10: 'to the intent that now the manifold wisdom of God might be made known by the Church to the principalities and powers in the heavenly places, according to the eternal purpose which He accomplished in Christ Jesus our Lord.' Verse 9 says that this was a 'mystery, which from the beginning of the ages has been hidden in God.'

So the Church's influence and effect has resonated in the heavenly realms, and will continue to do so. The Church's existence and purpose was kept hidden for ages and revealed in this age. The obvious inference here is that the Church was God's plan from the beginning, which He can now unwrap and present to a waiting world.

So God's strategy for the heavenly realms is through the Church. God's method for handling Satan's realms, his plans and strategies, is the Church. God's plan for the future is to bring glory to Jesus in the Church, throughout all generations for ever and ever. God's plan for your life is linked to the Church. God's plan for this generation, this country, this town, is in the Church. Have you ever wondered why comedy writers love to portray the Church and its ministers as weak, insipid, gutless, meaningless? Why does the media love it when some vicar or some minister falls sexually? The reason is simple – God's strategy on the earth is through the Church and Satan will do everything he can to demean it and destroy it. The truth is, the gates of Hell shall not overpower it. As we said before, no-one fights with gates! Gates are defensive. It is Satan's realm that should be defensive, not us.

That verse in Ephesians also gives us our strategic posture – the Church is not on the defensive but on the offensive. The Church's role is not to sit and wait and hope to defend. The Church's role is positive – gloriously positive and on the offensive.

The Church is described as 'the pillar and foundation of truth'. Spoken truth is supported, and given substance, by the Church. God does not have an alternative, this is the plan that is to work and will work. Look at Ephesians 1:22–23: 'And He put all things under His feet, and gave Him to be head over all things to the Church, which is His body, the fullness of Him who fills all in all.'

We are the expression on earth of His fullness. He has no other body to express it through except us – the Church. We are His arms, His legs, we are His physical presence on the earth. We are the light of the world, we are the salt of the earth – there is no other.

The Church is precious to God

The highest value God could place on anything has been placed on the Church. In Acts, Paul says, 'Be shepherds of the Church of God, which he made his own through the death of His own Son.' The price for the existence of the Church of God was the death and blood of Jesus. There is no higher price. In Timothy, we read that it is 'God's Church'.

In Revelation, the greatest possible term of endearment is

given to the Church – the wedding of the Lamb has come, and His bride has made herself ready. Blessed are those who are invited to the wedding supper of the Lamb. One of the happiest moments in life is hearing the music start and seeing a bride walking down the aisle. So He bought us with His blood – He calls us His, and He describes us as the bride getting ready for her marriage to the Lamb. What fantastic value God has placed on us, what security and reassurance there is in that for us!

The Church and me

There is no concept in the New Testament of a successful 'churchless' walk with God. The two appear contradictory. I need the Church and the Church needs me. You need the Church and the Church needs YOU! When we are born again (the Greek is 'born from above'), we are born to breathe heavenly air and the Church is our spacesuit in a world where there is no such air. Just like the astronaut, we need an appropriate environment if we are to survive. Cut it off and in seconds, minutes, weeks or sometimes months if we're fortunate, something within us dies.

If I try to pursue what I term my 'calling' or my part of the Kingdom of God – business, medicine, marriage, family, education – without the Church drenching, filling, supporting, or without total involvement, I will probably die somewhere along the route. It won't always be a dramatic, obvious death, but it will be the death of barrenness, dryness and scepticism – maybe the death of mediocre neutrality. Attending all the important functions, but with no heart in it.

In Ephesians, Paul cries out, 'that you may know to which he has called you – the riches of his glorious inheritance in the Son.' Paul makes it clear that we are called to the Church – the very word Ekklesia, 'called-out', reinforces it.

I am not called exclusively to education, to the shop-floor, to business, to politics or to social action. I am called to the Church, and in the Church I shall be equipped and sent out to do God's work in these fields. Supported, strengthened, encouraged, confronted, prayed over.

Paul goes on to make it clear that when we attempt to follow God's will, there will be warfare. Our struggle is not against flesh and blood but against the rulers, against the authorities, against the power of this dark world and against the spiritual forces of evil in the heavenly realms. You can't make it for ever on your own. In the prayer that was to be a model for every day, Jesus taught 'lead **us** not into temptation but deliver **us** from evil'. We are not called to handle these things on our own.

Whatever our area of function, it needs a supernatural wineskin to handle the supernatural realm that in reality we occupy. That wineskin is the Church.

George Eldon Ladd described the Kingdom and the Church as follows:

> The Kingdom creates the Church, works through the Church and is proclaimed in the world by the Church. There can be no Kingdom without a church (those who have acknowledged God's rule) and there can be no church without God's Kingdom; but they remain two distinguishable concepts – the rule of God and the fellowship of men.

I would add that there can be no concept of my calling to work without an immersion in church.

The Church as a source of identity

There are primary needs in every human being, including the need to belong relationally, and the need to know who I am functionally. Of course, my value, my worth, my relational need for love and total acceptance, is met primarily by God himself. But he has seen to it that is reinforced by his household – the Church.

In the Church another need is met, and that need is the need to know who I am functionally. The principle in scripture is clear – every member in the Church is gifted with one or more of the gifts of the Spirit and those gifts, when stewarded, will open ever-increasing horizons of function. It is these gifts that will often determine my role in wider areas such as business or education, and it is these gifts that will cause our beings to resonate with the sense that this is what I was created for. I am still shocked by the number of Christians in renewal/restoration who don't know what their gifting is and therefore miss a whole chunk of their function and identity.

Church is the source of our equipping

In Ephesians, Paul talks quite clearly about us 'being created in Christ Jesus to do good works which God prepared in advance for us to do'. Those good works can be a whole variety of things, but will certainly include our roles in our homes, business, education, family, social action and politics.

In the Church, God has appointed first of all apostles, prophets, teachers, miracle-workers, healers, administrators and so on. These gifts are the method by which Jesus builds the Church. With these gifts in operation we will lack nothing. These gifts are there to prepare God's people for works of service. The truth is that I will never be equipped or fully matured without these gifts building me up – strengthening, directing and encouraging me. This is so important to unity, to growth, to finding our function, to equipping others, so that God's Church can build itself up.

Every great man and woman of God became great because they selflessly stewarded the gifts that God gave to them. Christ feeds and cares for the Church. He makes her holy by cleansing her, by the washing of the water of the Word. We need to be what God wants us to be.

The Church as well as work is my crucible

As we saw in chapter seven, the crucible is the pot which exposes metals like gold and silver to intense heat, so that impurities float to the surface and can be scooped off. Paul explains this –

'we must go through many hardships to enter the kingdom of God, they said.' Paul and Barnabas appointed elders for them, in each church, and with prayer and fasting committed them to the Lord in whom they had put their trust. We talked just now about trials and tribulations, and the Church is a prime provider of these! My life is exposed by the confessing of sins and faults to one another. My life is confronted with teaching and prophecy in the Church. In the closeness of real fellowship I cannot escape or retreat from people, housegroups or circumstances that I find difficult to handle. God invests his elders and his shepherds with authority, and often that authority can cut across our will, our thoughts, our desires.

So the Church is a God-given environment for turning the heat up, forcing dross and impurity to the surface and scooping it off. Without the Church, I run the risk of losing all or part of this marvellous provision, leaving me incomplete.

A sitting lunch for wolves

Without the Church I am a sitting lunch for the 'savage wolves'. Paul says to the elders of the Ephesian church, in the context of his last words in the flesh to them, words to remember – 'I know after I leave, savage wolves will come in among you and will not spare the flock'. If we have an incorrect concept of, or an incorrect attitude towards, the Church, we are easy pickings for the savage wolves. Note the plural – *wolves*. As Jesus said, these ferocious wolves can come in sheep's clothing, so that you never know their identity until it's too late.

I love to visit the Savannah and Veldt areas of Africa whenever I travel there. I love to watch the majesty of the predators. I love to watch hunting dogs take down the mighty wildebeest. I love to watch the natural world documentaries on the TV. I was reminded of this chapter recently, when watching a pack of small wolves take down a massive and impressive buffalo. How do small, insignificant creatures take down such an animal? It is so simple. They watch for one on the edge of the herd. He is so self-assured, so confident that his strength is adequate! All they do is constantly nip at his heels. At first he hardly notices. Then he gets irritated and begins to kick back almost half-heartedly. Then they do it so constantly that they do not let him eat or drink. After several days, he begins to tire, and after a few more days he stumbles and the wolves have him. They sink their teeth into the neck, the blood spurts and it's all over.

I wonder if you are on the edge of the herd? I wonder if the wolves are already nipping your legs? I wonder if they have already stopped you eating and drinking? How will you know? Here are 10 Warning Symptoms:

1. A gradual and increasing pre-occupation with things outside the Church, to the increasing exclusion of the Church – in particular work or home.

2. Sterile, barren, fruitless, dry or dusty walk with God. Bible and prayer probably partly neglected, but apparently valueless! Heavens feel like brass.

3. Growing dislike of time with other Christians or growing reluctance to spend time with them.

4. Increasing retreat into your own world, which brings detachment, loneliness, isolation or independence. This is rarely wilful but by default. You probably don't actually like this experience, but find it difficult to force your way back into fellowship.

5. Increasing success in the area of pre-occupation.

6. Increasing wealth – less need of God and His Church; thanksgiving gets less and consumption gets more; giving out of guilt or increased stinginess.

7. Increased levels of temptation in areas like sex, materialism and new philosophies such as New Age.

8. No operation of the gifts of the Spirit.

9. Increased confidence and reliance on your own strength and your own abilities.

10. Where once you led God's people, you now sit in passive, mediocre neutrality.

If you will look now, you will see the eye of the wolf and smell his fetid breath. You may still have the chance to run back to God's Church. How do we do that in practice? We check our beliefs and examine what it means to be committed to our local church. We also settle our commitment to our churches' leadership and the issue of relating positively to other church members.

We will discuss in the next chapter how we do that in practice.

Chapter 9

SUPPORTING THE CHURCH WITH WORK-BASED SKILLS

There are two parts to this issue. The first one is – how to support? In one sense, this is the pivotal issue around which everything else will turn. There is an issue, a current issue, to be resolved in our minds – an issue in which I have already learned to die and where the cost has been faced. That is the place of the Church in my life. We looked at this together in the previous chapter. This issue will surface from time to time, and the frequency with which it surfaces will be directly proportional to the reality with which I have dealt with it!

The Church is the expression on earth of His fullness – He has no other body to express it through except us, the Church. We are His arms, His legs, His physical presence on the earth. We are the light of the world, we are the salt of the earth – there is no other plan. So, firstly, *I must thoroughly resolve the issue.*

I can't count the number of times a business person has told me things that they can see wrong in their church. They usually tell me with a sigh – a weary, 'why can't they see it?' kind of sigh. The implication is that their successful work environment, their earned respect at work, is somehow the basis for an automatic right to speak into the Church, see its faults and provide the remedies. The working person who has no real root in the Church, the working person who has not resolved that issue, is like a disconnected eye. You can see all you want, but you will never successfully communicate that back to the body because the effective connection is simply not there. The danger with that is that there will come an increasing estrangement. Damaging things are likely to be said, and if you are not very careful, a critical or cynical root will spring up and it will defile others.

It was said of the 90's that they would be a decade where Christians would part with everything except their time. That has proved to be frighteningly true. How about a challenge to bring our time under the Lordship of Christ? One way to do that is to ask God, in your times of prayer, to speak into what you do with your time. How about writing down what you feel He says? How about sharing that with the leader of your cell group, or your pastor or one of the elders? At Basingstoke Community Church, twice a year, the leaders take three days out for prayer and strategy review. As part of that review, each leader is required to share what his workload is and what he is doing with his time. It is a very healthy exercise and, nearly every time, one or other of us benefits from the corporate prayer and wisdom, and adjustments can be made.

One of the ways to get support if you are a busy individual, with a number of consuming responsibilities, is to sit down with your pastors or fellow leaders and say, 'Look, this is what I do. Here are my responsibilities. Please help me weigh them up – am I following God or am I being duped?' One of the most meaningful things you can subsequently do is to say, 'Look, this is the likely time I will have available. What are your priorities for the time that I can give?' In other words, let your fellow elders or your pastor have input into deciding what you give your time to.

How to support without threatening

This is the second part to this issue. There have been a number of times over the years where I have endeavoured to help in a church situation, only to sense some resistance. Being the sensitive soul that I am, I usually interpret that as rejection and my natural tendency is to say, 'Well, stuff it then!' and then go and withdraw.

What happened? In nearly every case it has been my attitude, the way I have come across, the spirit which I am operating in. Typically, in my case, I can come across as forceful, unyielding, impatient, arrogant, perhaps even condescending. Why would I be like that? Well, because I am expecting the same response as I would get in the office that I run, or from the clients who pay for my advice. They are two totally different spheres of government and I cannot approach one, necessarily, in the same way as the other.

Business can be so wonderfully pragmatic, so ordered, so structured. It is easy for me as a businessman to move in my own strength, my own authority. How is that reflected?

- Impatience with church members and their lack of commitment – particularly if giving happens to be down at the time!
- Impatience with church leaders and their inability to make decisions in a reasonable length of time.
- An arrogant devaluing of what they do – thinking that it is trivial.
- Rushing to get away from meetings because I have something more practical, more real, more valuable to do.

Very often the leaders in our churches have left well-paid, well-structured, re-assuring working lives, to take up the lowly-paid, insecure and fickle world of the Church. They don't have the money we do, they don't have the parameters of success that we so often have. They don't have a lot of things that we do.

If we could love them, if we could serve them with a serving heart, if we could commit our time to them in ways which are helpful to them, we could support them without threatening.

How to support without turning the Church into a business

In chapter five, we saw the role of Priscilla and Aquilla, Simon the Tanner, Paul, the Roman Centurion and Lydia. At the heart of each of these situations was a holistic view, not separating the so-called sacred from the secular, but treating both work and church-related functions as parts of one integrated whole. In essence all they did was to bring the whole of life under the Lordship of Jesus. They made the whole of their lives available to God with no strings attached, no ulterior motives, just a desire to serve God with the resources He had given.

The simple clue is to live or walk by the Spirit in our working areas, in the Church and in areas where the two intersect. If we have ears to hear, there is no demarcation line — it is simply walking by the Spirit with what God has given to us. If we can simply walk by the Spirit, we will have no danger of turning the Church into a business.

One of the simplest keys, one of the greatest acts of supporting the Church, is to function in spiritual gifts. They can, and should, flow regularly and routinely in our working environment, and they should also be one of our prime responses to the desire within us to support the Church. Those gifts will not turn any church into a business.

I know, from twenty years of travelling and preaching, that most churches would be radically transformed if all their members would obey the seven injunctions in 1 Corinthians 14, beginning with love — 'Pursue love, and desire spiritual gifts, but especially that you may prophesy.' The chapter goes on to state clearly that the use of gifts is to 'help build up the Church'. It is very uncommon to see any more than 20% of the members in the average church truly functioning in spiritual gifts. If we are not functioning in them in the church context, it is almost certain that we are not functioning in them in the working environment. If we are not functioning in them in the church context, the Church will not grow — that is a guarantee, even a promise. If we are not functioning in those gifts, then the load, the unbearable load, the crushing load will almost always fall on the elders, the leader, the pastor. That will lead to sterility, to limitation, to barrenness.

This is active serving. Bringing what we have, so that Jesus can build His Church. Coming to the Church with commitment

– commitment to its leaders and elders, commitment to work out my place in it and commitment to be an active, participating member and for that participation to include an active, violent, pursuing attitude towards spiritual gifts. An active participation that knows that when I contribute, then the 'Body builds itself up in love'.

How Jesus used his business experience to build his Church

I was speaking to Bill Cherry, of Netcom International, in his Australian base. Bill had made some very helpful comments on some of this manuscript. Bill was concerned, however, about some of the statements made about Jesus. When I outlined the following, it seemed to put his mind at rest, so let me share these thoughts with you –

In Jewish culture, it was said that a man was teaching his son to steal if he did not teach his son a trade by the age of twelve. We know from that, and from the reference in Mark's Gospel, that Jesus would have been apprenticed as a carpenter and was known for his activity in that realm. Most Bible teachers agree with the suggestion that Joseph probably died during Jesus' teenage years. That, by inference, would mean that Jesus, as the oldest son, would become self-employed – a micro entrepreneur – or at least a partner in the family business.

Jesus was known as the Son of Man. There are all kinds of theological ramifications to this! However, suffice it to say that He could have called on twelve legions of angels and didn't. He learned obedience through the things he suffered, He was tempted in all points like we are, and so it goes on. In other words, Jesus did not access the Divine nature. What it means in practice is that He came here as a man and He lived as a man. He dirtied nappies like any other baby. His body grew like any other man. Flames would burn Him, sun would heat Him. When He fasted, he grew hungry. He learned like other human beings. Of course there was destiny, of course He was the Son of God, but He was in human form.

Much of what He learned, He would have learned from the business environment. Where do you think He learned to understand people, read them and know them? Where do you think He learned to manage large sums of money which were evidently part of his later travelling ministry? Where do you think He learned to manage different configurations of teams?

George MacDonald put it like this:

> Jesus buying and selling! And why not? Did Jesus make tables and chairs perhaps, or boats perhaps, which the people of Nazareth wanted, without any mixture of business in the matter? Was there no transaction? No passing of money between hands? . . . No, there must be a way of handling money that is as noble as the handling of the sword in the hands of the patriot.

Where did He learn to pray? Where did he get His remarkable ability to understand ordinary men and women? Jesus was probably the superlative outdoor activity instructor, regularly putting His disciples into situations in the outdoors, which they would find difficult to handle. He taught them by exposure to face internal fears, to face external danger. He taught them to handle ministry success and failure.

The Son of God may have been supernaturally conceived, but clearly if He learned obedience through the things He suffered, He learned these skills and developed His potential through his place at work.

As a micro-entrepreneur, self-employed or as a partner, He would have faced so many of the pressures that business people face. He carried these attributes from work into church seamlessly. There was no secular barrier or line that He was afraid to cross. This is the Son of God. If it was so for Him, it can be even more so for us.

What were the ingredients that made it seamless for Jesus? He was there to do the Father's will. He utilised all the supernatural gifts in every environment and He supremely walked by the Spirit. These were the ingredients that enabled Him to learn or develop all these work-based skills and attributes. His Church was built with ingredients which involved their successful implementation.

The point to uncover and believe is that here is the Son of God, uniquely filled with the Spirit, with skill, ability and knowledge. These supernaturally endowed skills, abilities and knowledge were basic ingredients of His leadership, His discipleship and His Church's foundation and growth.

In an earlier chapter, we saw the first anointing of the Spirit. The scripture actually says, 'and He has filled him with the Spirit of God, in wisdom and understanding, in knowledge and all manner of workmanship' or, in the NIV translation, 'with **skill**, **ability** and **knowledge** in all kinds of crafts.' So the very first anointing was for practical skills, abilities and knowledge to be used in a church-based setting.

If we are filled with the Spirit, then our **skills, abilities** and **knowledge** can be profoundly useful. Ecclesiastes 10:10 says, 'If the axe is dull, and one does not sharpen the edge, then he must use more strength; but wisdom (or skill) brings success.'

Examples

There are all kinds of ways in which our Spirit-given work-based skills can bring success and save resources:

cell group leading, hospitality, intercessory prayer, evangelism, teaching, pastoring, counselling, accounting, fundraising, legal work, charitable work, copy writing, promotion, administration, stewarding, cooking, DIY, work with children and teenagers, pregnancy counselling, giving regularly and sacrificially.

Clearly this list is not exhaustive, and includes a mix of practical talents along with spiritual gifts. Peter Wagner has written an excellent book called *Your Spiritual Gifts Can Help Your*

Church Grow (Regal Books). I don't agree with every definition but it has been one of the most helpful books available in enabling Christians discover their gifting and put it to work.

Who is responsible?

Both working men and women and the church leadership are jointly responsible before God to steward their gifts, talents and resources. I would like to encourage church leaders to preach stewardship of time and resource, supernatural gifting and natural talent, and then call up church members to use their giftedness to the full. Where some kind of discipleship process is in place, I would expect accountability in these areas to form part of normal discipleship life. The cell group or home group is another outlet where this level of accountability can naturally take place.

Equally, every man or woman who has ever heard the parable of the talents knows the principle of putting your two to work to gain two more, and putting your five to work to gain five more. But bury the one that you have, in other words don't actively seek to put it to work in your local church environment, and then receive the following commendation from the Master – 'Wicked, lazy, worthless – throw him into outer darkness where there will be weeping, wailing and gnashing of teeth.'

For working men and women in the Church, God takes the principle of active participation – sacrificial participation – very seriously.

Giving

Once we have sorted the issue that our motive for work is not to provide for the Church, then it is a wonderful privilege to support by giving. I worked for years with Brian Rebbettes and John Rogers of Contract Leads. These two godly men taught me by consistent lifestyle the value, the privilege and the blessing of giving.

John Rogers had been taught at Covenanters by John Laing, the builder, and would often mention him to me with a knowing chuckle.

At the age of thirty, John Laing's business was in severe financial difficulty. He made a commitment to put God first in His life; God at the center of his life. He then set himself a financial plan which went like this, 'If income is £2000 per year, give £200, live on £500 and save £1300. If income is £4000 per year, give £1500, live on £500 and save £2000.'

When Sir John's will was published in 1978, his net estate totalled just £371. The man who had handled millions had given them away. You can travel in various parts of the world and see church buildings that owe their existence to John Laing's generosity.

I will never forget the moment when six of us in our early twenties carried a coffin into Basingstoke Baptist Church. Two weeks before, Jane Anderton had been with us as part of a young people's team to Kenya. She had been a brilliant contributor to the team's work. But she had contracted cerebral malaria and within a week or so went to be with the Lord. I remember carrying the coffin – I don't actually remember much about the service, but there is one other thing I remember well. When her personal effects were being given to her family, it was discovered that she had written cheque after cheque to different people in need. She was a giver. Up to that point, no-one had any idea about the extent of her giving. What a testimony, what a treasure and what a pleasure to God!

Jane was not a wealthy business person, she was a teacher. The point is that it doesn't depend on our wealth, it simply depends on our willingness to give what we are able to give – and in that way support the Church.

Chapter 10

REFLECTING REALITY IN OUR CHURCHES

If for decades we have been duped into falling for the sacred/secular myth, if for centuries our hearts and minds have been taught that the pastor and the missionary do the holy work, if for centuries we have been inseminated with the idea that certain types of work intrinsically carry more value than others, then it's little wonder that our churches don't exactly resonate with relevance to the average outsider. 'New' churches and traditional churches, it seems to me, vary little on this score.

This has combined with an ecclesiology – a view of church – which has tended to limit the belief of responsibility to neighbourhood contexts or foreign mission. Most of our congregations believe that we are the Church when we are together in the building, we are the Church when we are operating together in the neighbourhood, we are the Church when we are gathered together or when we are involved in foreign mission. But we are not the Church when we are scattered in the world. Then we are on our own. Individuals are salt, but they are not the Church!

Supporting working men and women

If as church leaders we won't change or don't change, then Christianity will become increasingly marginalised in the workplace, and our church gatherings and structures will become increasingly irrelevant to everyday people in normal occupations.

If the world of work is to be transformed, then something more than a developed doctrine of employment and vocation is needed. If not us, then who? If not now, then when?

For some of us, what we are reading in this book is new. For many of us, it is part of an ongoing impact that has been chiselling its way into our thinking. I really do believe that God has been speaking to us prophetically, and that inevitably requires some form of response.

Working men and women have a knowledge that there is more, a hunger to see more and in many cases a commitment to press through for more. How can we partner them? My question is this, can we change our practical support so that we can help to facilitate the integration of faith and work, so that our people feel their value and believe in the high calling of God, so they can live the gospel of the Kingdom, apply the gospel of the Kingdom and share the gospel of the Kingdom?

Can we find ways to encourage our workers in the convictions which they have that **work is significant, work is spiritual, work is holy and work is everlasting?**

Reflecting reality in Church structure

Before any specific changes are contemplated, the elders, the minister and team or the leadership team need to know clearly in their own minds what they believe and will need to discuss the implications. Change of thinking, real change of thinking, will require a change in response, in priorities and action.

Church notices are a mirror. They are a mirror into the reflected beliefs of those in charge. As I write this chapter, on my desk I have notices from various different churches – Salt & Light, Pioneer, Anglican, New Frontiers, Cornerstone, Ichthus, Catholic and New Life. I have counted 59 **pages** of notices in total, with just 39 **lines** that could be linked with the world of work. Those 39 lines take up less than one page. Compare that with 14 **pages** for the leaders' activities and prayer diaries, 21 **pages** of notices for meetings and 10 **pages** of items for sale.

How about starting here, ensuring that our notices include the world of work? How about a testimony from shop-floor, office or hospital ward? An encouragement each week on some work-related principle? While we are at it, how about a section each week devoted to the young people at school, college and university? And how about a sentence or two for unpaid workers like housewives or single parents?

Church meetings and gatherings need to be reviewed. All you leaders reading this chapter, would you think through this question with me? Our meetings – are they really there to serve working men and women, or are we deep down expecting **them** to serve **us** and the meeting? Perhaps it's a mixture.

At the Promise Keepers convention in Dallas, they asked the audience of 70,000 men to indicate if they had become a Christian through a church programme, or through the life and contact of one other individual. Over 80% reckoned to have come to Jesus through contact with one other person. Where are those people-contacts going to be? Please don't assume they are in the neighbourhood, because often they are not. For many of your congregation, the cell group is not the primary, or most logical, centre for evangelism. Could it be that you are going to have to change your concept of what meetings are there for? Imagine church support, in some way or other, for work-related groups, that gives out to people who almost certainly will never be members. In the next year or so, my prayer is that we will see this outworked in practice.

Leaders and their place in the world of work

I shall never forget the tears, the air of bleak disappointment mixed with the presence of God. One of my friends, who had had a thriving, successful business, had gone into liquidation that day. All the staff were being told and there were a few of us leaders from the church in the office to pray with, and support, the staff in their experience. It was a powerful time as we held hands together, church leaders and staff, and there were tears from Christians and non-Christians alike. There was an awesome sense of the presence of God involved in it all. That was, and still is to this day, a fairly rare experience. I don't mean the liquidation, but the mixture of church leaders with a business setting.

I know one or two church groups have had the occasional foray into world of businessmen. I'm all for that, but let's think of creative ways in which we could interact with all types of working men and women.

How about this excerpt from Charles Kingsley's *Life Letters*:

The people sprang to touch under the influence of the new rector – a man who feared no danger, and could steer a boat, hoist and lower a sail, shoot a herring net, and haul a seine as one of themselves. And when the herring fleet put to sea, whatever the weather might be, Mr Kingsley with his wife and boys would start down to the quay, and give a short parting service, at which 'men who worked' and 'women who wept', would join in singing the 121st Psalm out of the Old prayer book version, with the fervour of those who have death and danger staring them in the face. Such memories still make the name of Kingsley a household word in Clovelly.

In what creative ways could a pastor, minister or church leader adopt the same spirit or stance? I remember that for years my mentor and spiritual dad, Ron Trudinger, used to travel with me every week or so when I was a travelling salesman. He used to sit in the car while I made the visit, pray for a successful sale and then we would enjoy lunch or dinner together. Those days were memorable, we would laugh, we would pray, he would sharpen some area of my life, my work, my family or my preaching, and they were such enjoyable, productive days.

Working man or woman, in what creative ways could you invite some other church member to meet your colleagues, visit

your workplace, have lunch or whatever? Let's work together to
find a new creative way forward.

David Marchment, Senior Pastor at Basingstoke Community
Church, says:

> Having been a teacher for six years, I do remember well the pres-
> sures of that particular workplace. I often wonder, having served
> the Lord for twenty years in the employ of the church, whether
> regular time immersed in the 'marketplace' might be very good
> for all church staff, to help keep them informed and in touch
> with their congregations. Recently the local Baptist Church
> Pastor had a sabbatical and spent quite a bit of that time talking
> to 'all and sundry' in a local financial institution. He found it to
> be revolutionary to his understanding of where people are. He
> was shocked by the pressures many people are facing and had
> the opportunity to pray, and weep, with many of them!
>
> On occasions I have 'shadowed' members of the church for a
> day, and often arrange to 'visit people' at their place of work
> during the lunch-break. I have never failed to be thanked and
> appreciated when I have done this. Hazel, my wife, has done a
> similar thing with some of the ladies, and has been met with a
> deluge of thanks and requests for repeat visits!

Changing the way we preach

Our church gatherings are seldom, it seems, geared to the realities of the working men and women who attend them!

In chapter three, we saw that the under-35s rate the Church
as lowest of all in terms of relevance and trustworthiness, and
47% of church attendees rate the teaching as irrelevant to their
everyday life.

What can we do about that? The answer is simple – we must
preach like Jesus preached. Whenever Jesus preached, He
secured and held the attention of His listeners. He would estab-
lish a point of contact and then appeal to something familiar,
slap-bang up to date and relevant to the daily news or their own
realm of work or experience.

His messages were infused with regular, emotional life and experience. Jesus was regularly asking questions – over 150 in fact. Preachers, teachers and prophets reading this book, if we want listeners to respond to the answer we preach, we might be well advised to ensure that our answer is to a question they are asking or even a question they have the remotest interest in. If the common people heard Jesus gladly, He was addressing things that were of common interest. Consider just a partial list of the topics His preaching covered – adultery, death, debt, money, employees, employers, speech, stewardship, taxes, accounting, unkindness, virtue, zeal, anxiety, anger and divorce.

Jesus faced life and preached life in a gutsy, 'in your face' way. He drew vivid pictures from customs, family, employers, markets and shepherds. Ralph Lewis, in his brilliant book *Learning to Preach like Jesus*, makes this comment – 'The most famous preachers in two thousand years of Christian history incorporated at least some of Jesus' ingredients and preaching style.' He goes on to say of James Cox's book, *The Twentieth Century Pulpit and Twenty Centuries of Great Preaching*, 'Of the thirty-seven preachers Cox included, the sixteen popular and famous enough to be included also in the "Twenty Centuries" work averaged twenty-two questions per sermon.'

Those questions, if they capture real-life issues, were the same method by which Jesus taught with relevance. So, let's change the way we preach! Ralph Neighbour, in his cell-church model, recommends messages on contemporary issues for both non-churched and churched alike in the same meeting. Last year, I was invited to speak at Bombay Baptist Church in Colaba. I was given the title 'How to be successful in business'. The place was packed with many hundreds, including a good stack of non-Christians, both Hindus and Moslems. In fact, I was regularly interrupted by a vociferous Hindu, who was loving every minute and getting maximum value for himself. We spoke freely about Jesus and the Christian gospel, but it was also, both culturally and workwise, relevant to the congregation.

Changing the way we pray

Have you heard a minister pray over the offering, saying 'We often think of money as sordid, but you, Lord, have the ability to take what is sordid and turn it into something beautiful.' I remember similar prayers in my own experience of church in my youth. What does that say? What message does that send out?

Think of Laurie Deadman in my church, who has spent the week decorating people's homes. Think of Laurie Aldrich, who has spent a week, with overtime, working a lathe for Schlumberger. Think of Elaine Crick, a sister at the eye-clinic in Basingstoke. What would that prayer do for them, as they devotedly bring their tithes and offerings, having slogged their guts out in hard – and in the former two cases, manual – work?

We have tried to change this, at least a little, in our home church. At our last celebration, a large gathering of around one thousand people spent some time, as part of the worship, bringing tithes and offerings. Andy Kenward, one of my close friends, brought his tithe and we prayed together. We gave thanks for all the work God had provided over the last year. We prayed for continuing provision and prayed for the family, and there was a meaningful encounter between the two of us as brothers, and between both of us and God. Suppose, whilst praying with Andy, who has been patiently building his business through some very hard times, I had prayed 'God, take this sordid cash and bring usefulness in your Kingdom from it!' It would devalue his worth, devalue the sense of his calling and destiny in God and devalue his work.

Every time we take tithes and offerings, I am trying to make a habit of thanking God for the money, thanking God for employment and asking God for work for our unemployed. It can be very moving to have the unemployed come out for special prayer and bringing testimonies of prayer answered.

When you have a prayer time or an intercession evening, do you bring work-related issues into the prayer times? How about focusing on one group at a time, for example praying one evening for state school teachers, along with all the other issues? We did this a decade or so back in Basingstoke and within a few years every school had one or two Christian teachers. Some of our leaders today were born again at school events run by those 'prayed-in' teachers. We haven't prayed like that for years in our church! Shame on us.

How about bringing some variety into prayer times, like praying in large groups, led from the front, then breaking down into small groups and rotating those groups? Try to ensure that, each time, you pray for some work-related issues in those small groups.

In the cell-group or housegroup, why not get each man or woman – one per week – to share about their work, specific challenges or opportunities and important relationships? Pray for those areas regularly.

David Marchment again writes:

In twenty years I have had to handle, and seek to help, many who have struggled, in one way or another, with their working environment. The issues have ranged from excessive pressures and deadlines, to verbal, physical and sexual abuse. Yet, even with the knowledge of all of this, it's easy for church staff to be so focused on the running of the Church that church members, who are facing daily pressures in the work place, can so easily feel misunderstood, ignored, or even irrelevant or insignificant. I am grateful for the number of wise businessmen and women who have constantly challenged me, and kept me aware and focused. We can all wear 'blinkers' – but we need one another, and that fellowship where 'iron sharpens iron', to keep one another on our toes. I now really appreciate the opportunity of simply listening to people talk about their work situations, and want to take the time to pray for people, and bless them in the name of Jesus for all they are doing. It's wonderful to be able to take in the tithes and offerings, and then to pause to present them to the Lord, and to bless the people for their faithfulness, and pray for the unemployed. It can so often

be the case that the Church fails to appreciate the time pressures, and restraints that many people operate under. We can
perhaps heap pressure on, with our unrealistic demands,
simply because we fail to see that most people have already
been 'on the go' for some ten, twelve, or fourteen hours or
more! How necessary it is for people to be properly pastored,
where they know their unique situation is understood, appreciated and 'covered' in prayer! I've had guys call me to tell me
where they are going. They've told me of the pressures and
temptations that will be confronting them . . . Simply because
they know of their own vulnerability, and they long to be held
accountable – to be able to return home knowing they can say,
'there was temptation, but I resisted'. I am glad to be able to
thank God for such men, and my love and esteem for each one
has grown each time they have made themselves vulnerable.
I'm currently on a crusade to cut out all unnecessary 'stuff'.
I'm also learning, increasingly, to say 'no' to some invitations,
projects and other demands which, if I'm not careful, will
consume me. They can so easily crowd out our family time and
our time with the Lord. We all have to learn to govern, and
govern well, what has been entrusted to us so that as we walk
through the front door every evening, and eventually lay down
to sleep, we are not so 'wrung out' that we can't relate to our
loved ones, or even to the Lord.

Changing our language

I have really struggled with this one. With our own leaders, I
have tried for years to get them to stop using the phrase 'full-
time'. They do try, but it regularly slips back into the language
of the moment. It is easier than working hard to find a meaningful alternative. Just last night, in an elders and wives gathering, the phrase 'full-time leaders' was used on a circulated
document. I do try hard not to seethe! I requested again that we
ask the originators not to use the phrase. One of my pals, Dave
Downer, said, 'What do you call them then?' acknowledging the
practical need to have a working definition.

There are a number of choices, but how about 'church staff' or 'church-funded leaders'? I don't know what suits your environment best, but can I be allowed one coercive plea in this book? Good! Please determine you will not use the phrases 'full-time worker' or 'full-time leader' ever again. Thanks, I feel a bit better now! I tell you what, how about your church sending me £5 every time one of your team uses the phrase!! I could probably build a third-world clinic for my nursing daughter to staff in the first month of this book's publication! Any takers? . . .

Changing the teams that lead

I have been to more leaders' meetings than I've had hot dinners! Well, not exactly, but they do seem to crop up with incredible frequency. In the real world, the world where time is costed and weighed up in its use, meetings are quite interesting. I have just come from one of my clients this morning. We had a meeting of seven highly-paid men and women. We started at nine-thirty and by eleven I had finished the minutes. We had twenty-five action points – most of those will be actioned by the next time we meet, in another month's time. I then spent fifteen minutes with the M.D. talking about issues with six of his staff. Contrast that with the average church elders' meeting – four to six hours a week, with a budget a fraction of my client's. And if my experience from church audits is anything to go by, raising the same issues week after week, month after month and even year after year!

Now, don't shout at me! I know church is not a business, and we don't run it like one. Sure! Neither is the worship band a New Testament biblical model, but you wouldn't dream of using unskilled and ill-equipped musicians in your average church, now would you? So, how come musical skills are not suspect, but decision-making skills are? You might be thinking, 'Well, this is God's work and we need to do things gradually and we need to reflect and pray.' Please answer one question for me. Did you just assume, in my business meeting this morning, that I didn't pray? Are you assuming that my business meeting was somehow less important to God than my elders' meeting last night? Interesting questions, eh?

I am blessed to be to be included in prophetic teams and to be included in apostolic reviews. I really do feel properly received and valued by my church-based colleagues. I have a group of fellow-elders who have been committed to each other for nearly twenty years. They have welcomed me, they encourage me to bring my contributions and they listen – they really listen. They also tell me quite quickly when they think I am out of order! There are a handful of other working men in our eldership and I believe we are richer for it. When all you have on a leadership team or an eldership is church-paid staff, it can be incredibly unreal and not earthed. The inclusion of working men – not just businessmen – earths the team into reality. It is God's diversity for good reason. Why not allow one of your businessmen or consultants to share Edward De Bono's *Six Thinking Hats* as a means of making godly decisions? Prayer can be added, to make it 'Seven Hats'. It's not New Age, it's not some weird stuff – it's applied common sense from a very sound understanding of the human mind.

In case this makes you nervous, look up in any good commentary and see where the book of Proverbs originated. It is widely accepted that Solomon and other contributors took a number of these sayings – or the principles behind them – from other non-Jewish sources, in particular the Egyptian teaching of Amenemope. In other words, in our primary source of wisdom literature, the wise men borrowed, and then adapted freely, from pagan or non-Jewish sources. As Derek Kidner puts it, 'If Proverbs is the borrower here, the borrowing is not slavish but free and creative. Egyptian jewels, as at the Exodus, have been re-set to their advantage by Israelite workmen and put to finer use.'

Dear senior leader reading this chapter, make room – make room not just to be theologically correct, but ask the Father who are the working men and women that should be in your core team. You probably expect the businessman or woman to humble themself and accept church doctrine and practice. How about humbling yourself and accepting some practical down-to-earth wisdom?

Churches that have moved away from working men and women in their core teams will, in my view, suffer in their relevance, in their breadth and in their effectiveness. They will have a strong emphasis on doctrine and practice, but will lack elements of wisdom, prudence and faith.

Working man or woman, ask God how you can humbly offer the personal resources that you have. Don't get frustrated if you are not received for a season – let God use that to refine character and process.

Chapter 11

SEX

I bet some of you came to this chapter first!! One preacher used to tell the story of the advert in his local paper which had a headline like this:

> **SEX**
> Now that I have got your attention I have a car
> for sale!

I was awake early in my hotel room in Dallas, Texas. My friend, David Crick, and I had been running a seminar on sales skills and this was our weekend off. But I couldn't sleep. I got into the lift to get some breakfast and observed a lift full of men with Bibles. The time was 6 am. I asked what was going on and discovered there was a Promise Keepers' convention being held in the Dallas Cowboys' Stadium. These kind fellows gave us one ticket and sold us another, and David Crick woke up unexpectedly early, to find himself on the way to the big event!

It was staggeringly impressive, with around 70,000 men there for the express purpose of recommitting their lives to God, reaffirming their marriage commitments and praying for one another for marital fidelity. The movement clearly scratched an itch, because that one tour alone, with some twenty-two venues, had seen 1.2 million men attend! When they did a survey of the most common problems these men experienced, I heard it reported that 600,000 referred to the issue of sexual temptation as the number one problem in a walk with God.

You might be forgiven for asking why on earth there is a chapter on sex in a book about work! I'll tell you why – clearly. It is the number one source of seduction and destruction at work. It is also one of the most common of all temptations and very few Christian working men and women, or their churches, talk openly enough about it.

As I was preparing material to write this section, a leader in a UK church was arrested for child pornography on the Internet. The same week, I had a visitor from another nation and in my questioning it transpired that he had seen videos in a hotel room that were of a sexual nature. A few days later, I had a call from another man somewhere else who had been surfing Internet pornography for weeks, for hours at a time. A day later, a young Christian leader called me to share some problems with sexual temptation in the realm of thought life and fantasy. All that in just one week! But that is not unusual, and all these men were godly men wanting to do His will in their lives.

This is the number one robber of men, marriage and ministry, and increasingly so for women. The sobering truth is that any one of us can fall. David was a man after God's heart and yet he committed the murder of one of his most faithful men in order to fondle the body of his wife.

David fell, amongst other reasons, because he had begun to rest on his previous successes. Possibly because he had been advised to stay at home, he began to wonder about his own feelings of worth, value, manhood and identity. Whatever the real reason, instead of going out to war, he was staying back at home. My guess is that he had previously seen her body from a distance, and the secret places of his heart were already planning the move.

He paid a frightful price – although there was forgiveness.

Joseph was a brilliant contrast. Sin presented itself and he did the only thing you can safely do in a situation like that, and that is to run.

I remember queuing for the Alien ride at Disneyworld. The warnings about bad backs, nervous disposition and heart trouble added to the suspense in the long wait. I remember wishing I had all of those so that I could legitimately back out! Finally, Joel and I were there, strapped in the front row right by this huge glass cylinder. The story droned on, the music accentuated and suddenly, in front of us, the glass cylinder shattered and an alien was on the loose. The ride includes simulated dripping blood and the literal feel of the alien's breath on your neck – all in the dark and strapped in with no escape!

In the movie of '*Alien*,' the eggs get planted into humans. They are unaware of the fact, until at some point the invisible and imperceptible life-sapping force explodes out, and something very ugly and very difficult to deal with is set loose. Sexual desire can be just like that. If it is not dealt with at the root, then sooner or later it is going to hatch and what was whispered in the bedroom will be shouted from the rooftop. I was in the Crucible Theatre in Sheffield at a Spring Harvest leaders' conference, listening to Pete Meadows interviewing Jimmy Bakker. The pain of the man was evident, but so was the pain of the Body of Christ in the room. If Satan can take down a leader anywhere in the Body of Christ, then he has truly scored a victory – sheep are scattered and there is an ebbing in the force. My encouragement, men, is not to view it just as temptation but to view it as Satan's strategy loosed to bring down men and women of God. The book of Proverbs puts it this way, 'The adulteress preys upon your very life.'

Ladies, as Gill and I have talked and counselled with couples over the last ten years, my feeling is that sexual temptation is on the increase for you. But the most common, related area for women is romance. That housegroup leader who listens to you, and listens for long periods. That pastor, who actually understands you and speaks kindly to you. That non-threatening arm around you in the Church service. These will often be your danger points. The keys and the solutions are the same for both.

General keys to temptation

The Greek word which we translate as temptation in the Bible means that which puts us to the proof whether by good or malicious design. Another way of describing it is that the process of temptation 'assesses' what is there. One of the phrases *'peirasmod'* in the Greek means *'trials or testing with a beneficial purpose and effect'*. So we don't need to view temptation negatively or with fear. Temptation is **testing** designed to bring out what is really there in our hearts, as part of the process of maturing. Temptation is **proving**, designed to prepare us to receive what we long to be and what God has called us to be.

As we saw earlier, temptation is another crucible, where heat is applied until the dross surfaces and is skimmed off until the craftsman sees his face.

It is easy for us to have a negatively coloured impression when we hear or use the word *temptation*. My prayer is that together we can see and understand the positive power of temptation, as God filters it into our life to bring proving and maturing.

In the temptation of Jesus, there are three important statements which lead us to a very practical point – *full of the Spirit, led by the Spirit, tempted by the devil*. Temptation is not a sin. Say it as you read this! **Temptation is not a sin**. The understanding of this is fundamental to our victory. So many Christians have guilt and condemnation when they experience the thoughts or when they hear the devil's attractive suggestions. How we handle it will determine whether there is sin or victory – but *temptation itself is not sin*. The writer to the Hebrews makes it clear that Jesus was tempted in every way just as we are – yet without sin. So be encouraged – temptation is **not** sin. Satan uses a number of lies to defeat God's people. We will call this Lie Number One – don't believe it!

The devil is the tempter. Matthew's account clearly refers to Satan as 'the tempter'. We also have the capacity for our own 'evil desires' to draw us away and entice us, as James clearly states. How we handle the tempter from outside, or the desires from within, will determine whether it is sin or not.

Three lies from the tempter

1. Temptation is Sin. We have already seen quite clearly that temptation is allowed by God, has been experienced by Jesus and will be used by the Holy Spirit for our benefit to test us and strengthen us. He was tempted in all points just as we are, yet without sin.

2. It's only me! I'm the only one bad enough to have this sexual temptation, this financial temptation, this bitterness, this temptation to lie or to gossip. I must be very bad, very unspiritual – no-one else in this church has this weakness. It's a lie! 1 Corinthians says, 'No temptation has seized you except what is common to man.' Every temptation, even the most simple or the most wicked, is experienced by other men or women – you are not especially wicked, you are especially normal.

Get numbers 1 and 2 wrong, and you will experience feelings of guilt and condemnation. You need to recognise these feelings as temptation and deal with them – they are not the truth. 'There is therefore now no condemnation . . .'

3. I can't cope! Oh, yes you can! God promises you can. God is faithful and will not let you be tested beyond what you can bear. But when you are tempted, He will also provide a way out so that you can stand up under it.

Of course it is possible to choose deliberately to sin and then to fall increasingly to temptation. But when our choice is for God, God has promised it will never be beyond our ability to cope and that there is a way of escape!

How do we handle it?

1. Share It

In the disciples' prayer, Jesus did not say, 'Lead *me* not . . .' No, Jesus said, 'Lead *us* not into temptation' and 'Confess *your* faults one to another and pray for *one another*'. Major temptation is not meant to be handled on our own – when we share it we are halfway to victory. If you have a regular temptation or habit that is troubling you, in many cases you will not break it until you share it. It is not failure or weakness to need help, it is part of the humbling, true knowledge that we cannot cope in our own strength. I cannot recall a situation anywhere in the world where this process has failed, providing there has been ongoing, honest and on-time sharing.

> 'If you think you are standing firm, be careful that you don't fall.'

> 'Restore him gently, but watch yourself or you also may be tempted.'

2. Pray It

Jesus gave us a model prayer which is for daily use and temptation is a core element. This prayer model has changed my prayer life, in particular this phrase 'Lead us not into temptation, but deliver us from evil'. These are not idle words – these are life-changing truths. When I pray, the level of daily temptation is almost always perceptibly lower. When I don't, it's not too long before I link an increase in temptation with an absence of prayer. In Matthew, Jesus says, 'Watch and pray so that you will not fall into temptation.' The spirit is willing, but the flesh is weak – and prayer strengthens both.

Our present and future capacity for God is affected by our daily prayer. Our strength is affected by prayer. Temptation is a divinely given barometer for which we can thank God.

3. Define it, and deal with it by the Word of God

When it comes at you, say,

> 'This is **stealing**. It is **sin** – *"you shall not steal".'*
> 'This is adultery. It is sin – *"guard yourself in spirit and do not break faith".'*
> 'This is love of money. It is sin – *"keep your lives free from love of money".'*
> 'This is pride. It is sin – *"humble yourselves under the mighty hand of God".'*
> 'This is lust. It is sin – *"flee youthful lusts".'*

The 'Word' is crucial, because often we will not sense His presence.

These are the benefits of temptation –

1. It gives us an accurate mirror of where we are with God.
2. It strengthens our spiritual muscles.
3. It forces us into faith.
4. It calls us up into daily prayer.
5. It calls us up into daily use of God's Word, forces us into the well-spring within us and forces it onto our lips.
6. It teaches obedience.
7. We can experience forgiveness every time we fail (When we fall or fail, if we confess, He forgives).
8. Jesus is close to us at that point – 'We have a High Priest who has been tempted in every way, just as we are yet without sin. Let us, then, approach the throne of grace with confidence, so that we may receive mercy and find grace to help us in our time of need.'

Understand that sex is beautiful

Understand that sex is beautiful. God made it, He is not embarrassed about being in our bedrooms when we make love and the

Bible is full of it. Strange, isn't it, that the religious spirit that tries to make us view sex as dirty, ungodly and shameful is the same religious spirit that will cause us to have hidden extramarital sex when our issues are not resolved?

What does the Bible teach?

The scripture is full of instructions, guidelines, promises, warnings, consequences and blessings all related to sex. Song of Solomon – whatever its alternative theological significance – is erotic poetry at its finest. What a loving God, who includes, at the very heart of scripture, poetry that can raise the act of physical love to a height where it can be included in inspired writing. That fact alone, with no other evidence, would lead us to understand that God views human lovemaking as an inspired part of His creation, something clean and pure enough to include in his handbook for His creation.

The book of Proverbs talks freely about intimacy, and in describing ways to avoid immorality, encourages men to find intimate satisfaction from their wife's breast and talks about being 'captivated by her love'.

Biblically speaking the act of lovemaking is divinely conceived, divinely created and meant to be enjoyed. Whilst the Bible makes it clear that sex is meant to be enjoyed, it is equally clear that there are some boundaries. In an age of unrelenting pressure and exposure, the biblical absolutes are not a straightjacket of unnecessary restriction, but a source of utter release and relief.

Sexually activity is **not hidden** in scripture, it is not taboo nor is it regarded as embarrassing or smutty. The Bible does not hide its comments, positive or negative – it is plain. It talks about different types of kissing, it talks about nakedness, it talks about the erotic nature of the breast. It also spells out unequivocally what the boundaries are, and what the consequences are of crossing those boundaries.

Sexual intimacy was God's intention from the beginning. Mark's gospel says:

But from the beginning of the creation, God 'made them male and female.' For this reason a man shall leave his father and mother and be joined to his wife, and the two shall become one flesh. So they are no longer two, but one flesh. Therefore what God has joined together, let not man separate.

This is Jesus referring back to Genesis and making it clear that both old and new covenants alike were blessed with physical oneness at the heart of marriage. Notice that no children are mentioned here. In other words, the act of *one flesh* is an activity that stands in its own right. Whilst we know that children are a blessing from God, the sexual act is not just for the procreation of little ones!!

Whenever I am invited to preach more than one session, I always try somewhere or other to talk about sex and sexual temptation. Why? Well, it's not because I am particularly obsessed with the issue, it is because there has been a religious reluctance to talk about the subject and a seeming difficulty to deal with it without embarrassment. I have been preaching that way for at least fifteen years. On nearly every occasion men have come to me afterwards, or later on, and confessed some difficulty with pornography or the Internet, or with masturbation. It needed someone to open the door. I find it disappointing that it needs someone from outside to open the door. But folks, please let's talk about it, in church, out of church, at work and above all in the home.

When you are in the bath or shower, thank God for your body and the pleasure you and your spouse have from sharing physical intimacy. The Jews are better at this than Christians. They have prayers for different areas of life – they even have a prayer for thanking God for successful bowel movement. That is not a joke – it's part of appreciating what a wonderful body the creator has given us and thanking Him for its working order. We might well have better health if we could develop thanksgiving more as a way of life.

So let's be open, let's enjoy our sexuality, but let's be clear on the biblical boundaries without compromise.

Essential keys for handling sexual temptation

1. Open, honest, vulnerable, self-revealing and volunteered sharing

That heading is a mouthful but it is quite deliberate. There are five steps here, and this is where we will win or lose the battle for sexual purity –

i. Open. This means we determine from now on that we will not hide our problems or temptations. We begin to see hiding as an enemy in itself and we declare war on it. One of the enemy's most successful strategies with sex is to convince men and women that it is simply too shameful to share. I want to see this reversed so that we believe it is shameful **not** to share and very normal and natural to share. That means, for most married couples, that you determine to share every issue relating to temptation with total transparency. I say *'for most couples'*, because I believe that to be the best. I am, however, aware of relationships where that can be simply too painful for the wife. In these cases, the man must have a willingly open relationship with another mature Christian brother. *Open* also means that, as a fundamental pre-requisite, we have settled the issue that we cannot handle temptation on our own. *'Lead us not into temptation'* means exactly what it says. So we have now determined that for the rest of our lives we are going to be open about sexual areas with a pastor or a mature Christian that we trust – someone who will not just say, 'There, there!', but someone who will hold us accountable. *'Confess your faults to one another, pray for one another that you may be healed.'*

ii. Honest. This means what it says. When we confess our temptation or sins, we tell it like it is. I was staying away alone in a guest house in a remote part of Sweden. I had been away for some days and that evening, after finishing my consultancy with a nearby company, I sat down for my meal. The meal was superb, the place itself very romantic and I was totally on my own. There were no other guests and no other diners. The waitress, an extremely beautiful woman, came over and slowly handed me the menu, keeping her eyes on me and keeping her hand on the menu in such a way that it would touch mine. As soon as our hands touched, I knew something was happening but even so my reaction was not immediate. My hand stayed there for a few seconds and the feeling was pleasant. Nothing like that had ever happened before – it had taken me by surprise. I struggled with guilt for the rest of that meal and for some time after. When I came to share the situation with another Christian leader, I found an inner reluctance to be really honest. I could have fudged it. One part of me wanted to tell him a half-truth, something like, 'I was put into an awkward situation where a pretty waitress was looking suggestively at me.' Why the inner struggle to talk about the fact that our hands had touched? I am not absolutely sure, but I know that if I had not got the honest facts out, the same thing could have happened again. Honesty defeats that particular sin for the moment and puts stronger moral fibre within, to prevent anything similar happening again.

iii. Vulnerable. This simply means that we come to another brother or leader without preconditions. We let them steer the conversation as they wish and we make ourselves submissive in the process. I am reminded of a story I heard of a Christian in Canada, who was on a work assignment away for a day or so with another woman from the office. She was a Christian woman, so imagine his surprise when her hand rested on his leg as they were driving along! He did not immediately resist as she began to tell him how unhappy she was, how insensitive her husband was and how sensitive **he** was. He didn't say anything, but stopped at the next garage and made a phone call to the pastor. He climbed back into the car and she asked, 'Was that an important call?' 'Yes,' he replied. 'How important?' she asked, more concerned this time. 'Very important,' he replied. 'Well, what was it?' she said. 'I was calling my pastor to ask him to pray for me, and I told him I had a woman seducing me in the car.' The seduction stopped immediately! Thank God for this man's vulnerability and thank God for his pastor's wisdom. Vulnerability means you can't always be sure of the outcome of your open sharing.

iv. Self-revealing. This means we go out of our way to detail the truth, rather than waiting for it to be dug out. Over the years I have observed that people with habitual sexual sin find it very difficult to be self-revealing. The reason is often that they don't actually want to give up that sin, and the lack of self-revealing is a symptom of a hardened heart or a fearful heart that does not want to give too much away. Self-revealing means we reveal the detail quickly so that the sinful acts – like an uprooted weed exposed to the sunlight – rapidly wither away.

v. Volunteered. This means that we go out of our way to share or confess. We don't wait for special meetings and we don't wait for a pastoral check-up, we share – and the sooner we can do that the better. One of the young men in a local church asked me if he could call me any time he felt particularly vulnerable in the realm of sexual temptation. Sure enough, over the following six months, I had three or four calls on my answerphone. No details, obviously, but I knew what the calls meant. Because of business commitments at the time, I wasn't able to return a single call promptly but in each case the call itself and the volunteering of information had been enough.

2. Always share when you are away on your own

I was woken up one night with a call from Japan. A brother in one of our churches was feeling lonely, feeling slightly vulnerable and on his own. Would I pray for him to stand firm? What a pleasure to do that! I felt so proud of him, so privileged to be asked to stand with him. Once he had made the call, the possibility of sexual temptation was shared and dealt a death blow. I have made it a guiding principle with any of the men I have worked with, that when we are going to be on our own, we plan to share and we plan ahead with our pastor or friends to let them know that we will be sharing. Gill, my wife, expects me to communicate on the issue of sexual temptation along with all the matters for communication when I am away. In fact, she might even prompt me by asking me a question that gets me talking.

3. Set yourself some ground rules

You know where the danger areas are. I have one friend who was so tempted by hotel videos that he would take a screwdriver with him to take off the plug and then call one of us to confirm that he had done just that. I don't know many people who need to do that. We have tried over the years to make sure that no married men travel on their own with just one woman in a car. Where we live, it is twelve miles out from the main church building. It has often been the case that a wife wants to go to a meeting which I am travelling to alone. They know now that I will not take them alone in an empty car. Extreme? I am thinking right now of a man, a real servant in the church, who has left his family and has a relationship with another woman from the same church. When I think of his saddened wife and kids, I think I am probably not extreme enough. However, I am aware that it is not always possible to avoid this situation.

On a recent mixed church audit team, men and women were working together and occasionally travelled together. What can you do in a situation like that? Simple, keep open communications so that everyone knows who is going where, and when. I was away last year on a ministry trip with a team from Derby and Basingstoke. On the way home, it suddenly dawned on me that, on the last leg of the journey, I was going to be driving on my own at midnight with a single girl. What I did was to make a point of ringing home several times on the mobile, without making some big deal of it, letting them know where I was and when I was due home.

In business today we may often be required to spend time travelling away, even overnight, with members of the opposite sex. Some of you men may well have a woman as a boss and be in a situation where you are away with her. One of my friends was doing some work for a client, and at the first meal, in a group context, she showed the condoms she had with her in expectation of things to come. That was some years back – things are likely to be even more 'free' today. We do not need to be intimidated or even religiously prudish. It is an opportunity to talk about faith and sex – God's view of sex. And equally to make sure you have prayer cover and pre-determined times for accountability.

4. Plan to run and plan to avoid specific areas or situations

Joseph ran, and I think he ran because he had thought through the possibility ahead of time.

5. Know the triggers and take responsibility for them

What are your triggers? Alcohol? Alcohol will always lower moral guard, so be aware of how much you are drinking and in what setting. Loneliness, tiredness and particular colleagues at work can also be triggers. Success at work or in some church-related ministry can often lower our guard. As you read this, ask the Lord, 'What are the things that trigger sexual tempta-tion for me?' and take responsibility. Have a plan which you chat through if necessary, which enables you to plan to avoid, and enables you to plan to run.

6. Keep the door open

Never have a closed door in your house or office when you are on the Internet. Never shut the door when you are counselling or alone with someone of the opposite sex. And if you feel this is all too much, then let me remind you of what Paul said,

7. 'Let him who thinks he stands take heed lest he fall'

If we defend the existence of these situations in our lives, they become a stronghold and the urge will become a surge.

Can I ask you with all of my heart to resolve now to go and share, to be open, to be vulnerable, to be self-revealing, to confess your weaknesses? I have watched hundreds of men and women do this over the years. They haven't been rejected, they haven't been treated with shame and contempt – they have been loved and encouraged back to full spiritual health. Would you write down now, on this page or on a piece of paper, who you will talk to and when you will do it? Would you do that now? Thank you, God bless you and God Himself will set you free.

Chapter 12

MONEY!

The first question

I have asked this question all over the world. On this particular morning, I was asking it of leaders and congregation in a wooden building on the outskirts of Harare, Zimbabwe. Hilary Clinton visited this very building with one of the leaders' wives the week before! Here was the question: 'How many of you here believe that money is the root of all evil?'

I wonder what your answer was. Most of the congregation kept their hands down and looked at me smugly, as if to say, 'Okay, preacher, we have got your number, nice try, but we're not falling for that one!' And, as most of you know, they were right – it is one of the most commonly misquoted scriptures ever! It is the **love** of money that is the root of all evil.

The big one

In the laughter and fun that followed, I asked them another question. Let me ask you the same one. Here it is: 'How many of you here would like to be rich?'

This time, just about everyone's hand went up, including most if not all of the leaders! In fact I have asked this question scores of times, and around 80% of the average audience –

leaders included – put up their hands. Let me tell you what I told my friends in Harare that morning. Those of you that raised your hands are on a six-step downhill slide to destruction, defined quite precisely in 1 Timothy 6:9.

They looked at me, hoping I was winding them up and then we began to read this passage together. Would you be kind enough to get your Bible and read this section with me, as we highlight the six steps. Could you do that now please?

1. Fall into temptation and a trap
2. into many foolish and harmful desires
3. that plunge men into ruin and destruction
4. for the love of money is a root of all kinds of evil
5. some people eager for money have wandered from the faith
6. pierced themselves with many griefs

A true story

I want to tell you a true story from another country. I knew a para-church organisation which was into the discipleship movement. It was well known to the Spring Harvest leadership team. The leader had chosen his men carefully. Each of them could teach well and they had carried out successful deliverance and healing. Every one of them had a strong professed love for the Lord, and they worked well as a ministry team together. They had occasional differences – but seemed to work through them quite well.

One of the guys was given the responsibility of the cheque book, banking and petty cash. He kept good accounts, but seemed to have a bit of a mean streak. One night, at a fellowship outreach meal, one of the congregation gave a very costly present to the leader as a 'thank you'. The treasurer was furious. 'What a waste of money,' he said, 'Why don't we sell the thing and put the money towards our outreach programme for the poor?' In his unresolved fury, somehow or other he got involved in the occult. He got so mad that a few days later he phoned up the secret police, became an informer and got six months' salary up-front. The leader was subsequently arrested, tortured and, finally in this sad story, executed.

Afterwards, when it was too late, the treasurer got sick of himself and sick of what he had done. He gave the police their cheque back and went away and committed suicide.

It's a sad story – but it's quite frightening in the sense that it could potentially happen to any one of us!

The leader was well known to most of you – his name was Jesus. Judas was the treasurer. Here is what is so frightening. He was selected from a night of prayer. He could heal and cast out demons – probably even raise the dead. He could sit intimately close to Jesus at supper and, even at that moment, dip his bread into the same dish as Jesus. That custom is still current today in the Arab world – it means, 'I'm your friend; you can trust me.' But within seconds Satan had entered his heart and we know the rest.

Outwardly he was a good disciple. He had genuine faith, genuine relationship and genuine supernatural gifting. He was a good businessman with some very strong principles and moral standpoints. But he had a secret love and that love was money. In John's gospel we discover that he used to take money – literally sneak it from God's pocket!

How could he do that? Because he had a love for money that he kept hidden. The other disciples had their flaws, their mistakes, but they were open. Peter, James and John were open, and because of that their weaknesses could be adjusted and the process of humbling could take place. But Judas' love of money was so well hidden that no-one knew for three years. He was not self-revealing.

In that secrecy, the sin grew worse and the cancer took hold. He could still sing the songs, run the meeting, deliver people from demons. But because part of him was hidden, he fell into a trap. He got many foolish and harmful desires, and because they remained hidden they plunged him into ruin and destruction.

He was seduced by money and fell in love with it, and as he got eager for it he lost his faith and finally took another person's life and then his own. Literally 'pierced with many griefs'.

If he could have opened up and shared his weakness, if he had cried for help and repented, he could so easily have been saved. James makes it clear: 'Confess your trespasses to one another, and pray for one another, that you may be healed'.

Luke points out that 'you cannot serve God and money' and 'if you do not give up everything you have you cannot be my disciple'.

We know from the rest of the New Testament that it that doesn't mean 'no possessions ever', but it does mean that they don't possess you.

How can we tell if this cancer is in our bodies?

1. If you believe that godliness is a means to financial prosperity – it's a lie, it's a delusion, it's a deceit.
2. If you tithe, or give, in order to get back.
3. If you find it difficult to give often, readily, cheerfully and sacrificially.
4. If you say that you're in business to make money. There's nothing wrong with making money – it's a sign you are doing things right – but it should never be our goal or motive. It is a fruit, not the root. I'm in business for God and His kingdom, and I expect to be fruitful.
5. If you are stealing in any form – time, measurement or units.
6. If you are hiding any areas of finance that need confessing.
7. If you are lying about your finances.

The New Testament church were so shocked by Judas' financial sin that Ananias and Sapphira were struck down dead for lying over their finances. Why? Because Peter had had enough of disciples who lied about their finance. He had had enough of Christians who pretended to be truthful but were not fully self-revealing. The Bible calls that level of deceit *lying to the Holy*

Spirit. Isn't it interesting that the problem area for Judas and the problem area for Ananias and Sapphira was money?

Let's determine to be truthful, honest, easy to correct and self-revealing. I had a fascinating experience some years back. During my devotional time one morning, I felt God say quite clearly that I was to set a limit on my earnings and give half of the rest away into ministry of one kind or another. I wrote it down in my prayer diary and set up an Excel spreadsheet to do the calculations. It all seemed okay. But I noticed a change in my attitude. I no longer had any motivation to work – it all seemed such a drudge. I found anger surfacing in me every time I did the spreadsheet calculations. What was going on? God was revealing a hidden motivator and the hidden motivator was money! When I couldn't get all that I was earning, it took away the impetus to earn and my real motives were exposed!

What about prosperity?

Jesus has redeemed us from the curse of the law. Poverty was a curse under the law, so we are redeemed from that. 'Blessing' simply means 'more of what you have got that is good'. That includes both the material and spiritual. Listen to these words taken from God's directives to the people of Israel:

'I will bless you in all your work and in everything you put your hands to.'

'The Lord your God will bless you in all your harvest and in all the work of your hands and your joy will be complete.'

'The Lord your God will make you prosper.'

Interestingly, in each of these cases, the blessing was not for self-indulgence – it was a reward for 'faith in action', as the Israelites did things for one another, and for God, that made no financial sense. These things included lending freely, cancelling debts and spending three weeks a year dedicated to appearing before God with no work being done. Whatever else the prospering of the Israelites entailed, it was not primarily for self-consumption.

Prosperity versus materialism

Prosperity is both spiritual and financial. Prosperity means the well-being of spirit and soul as well as money, goods, food and possessions. It is not the same as materialism. Materialism says, 'I want more, I want more **now,** I want what they have got, I want what I cannot afford'. Religious materialism says, 'I will be godly and apply the rules of the Bible in order that I may be prosperous'. The outcome of that may or may not be a fact, but the motive is impure. James makes that clear when he says, 'You ask and do not receive, because you ask amiss, that you may spend it on your pleasures'. As we saw in an earlier chapter, if we seek first the kingdom, all these things will be added. Remember the mathematical term **'added'.** Not multiplied. It implies a process, line upon line, little on little. Proverbs even says, 'He who gathers money little by little makes it grow'. Prosperity is seen as a process. Prosperity is also for the soul and includes well-being, whereas materialism is the pursuit of possessions. So we can expect godly prosperity to carry with it the ability to enjoy with peace what God has to give. Ecclesiastes puts it like this: 'As for every man to whom God has given riches and wealth, and given him power to eat of it, to receive his heritage and rejoice in his labour – this is the gift of God.'

So we could define prosperity as something not to be pursued, but as something which God adds, rather than something we take. And prosperity includes the gift of God to enjoy what we have. If we are kept in a constant place of need, then we need to check our attitude – God may be keeping us there for a reason.

Prosperity involves stewardship

Prosperity is for stewardship, not for self-consumption. That is not to say that possessions are intrinsically wrong or unspiritual.

Nor does it mean we have to adopt a lifestyle of poverty. Jesus had no place of His own, yet he had a coat of value that was gambled for because of its quality. He had no problem receiving perfumed lotion costing £25,000 or more in today's values. He could also say, 'You cannot be my disciple if you don't give up every thing you have'. And he could also say to the rich young ruler, 'Sell all you have and follow me'. That is not contradiction, it is truth in tension. What we own, and are blessed with, is there for us to steward – for our lives, for our families, for the poor and for the Kingdom of God.

Our family has known times of great financial hardship and we have known times of plenty. The challenges of both are different, but the reality of God and His presence are the same in both. I can remember Gill sitting on the stairs crying because we did not have enough money to buy shoes for our children. I saw the joy in her eyes last week as we were able to give to Tear Fund for its Balkan appeal. God has been in both.

I know a number of successful men and women who feel the need to justify their wealth, by implying that the reason they are running a business is so that they can fund a specific project or church or whatever. That is a wonderful outworking of stewardship, maybe, but it is not why they are working. As we saw before, it is fruit, not root. If you read Hudson Taylor's biography in two volumes, the role of one prominent business-man surfaces time and time again. Without him, Taylor would not have done all that he did do. But this man did not go into business in order to finance Taylor – it was the fruit of his stewardship. Why the emphasis on a seemingly minimal distinction? Because that distinction affects motives and it affects the desire, or need, to have control and those can become very big and very damaging issues in the Body of Christ.

Chapter 13

GIFTS AND MINISTRIES IN THE WORKPLACE

The Bible indicates clearly that there are days ordained and there are works ordained – there is an 'appointment' already written into our beings before we are created. This is one reason why, as Christians, we often get a strong inner restlessness – a godly dissatisfaction. These days, these works and these appointments are like a Divine magnet, pulling us strongly to fulfil all that we were created to do. These appointments, these days and these works are what we were created to do. They are like a vacuum sucking us constantly and consistently, wanting to be filled. In Psalm 139, God talks about *'knitting us'* with stitches that contain the blueprint of this function, our ministry and our destiny. If you like, a spiritual DNA.

This spiritual DNA has in it, not the colour of our hair or our eyes, but who we are in God. God has programmed into us gifts, actions, deeds and destiny. When I am born again and filled with the Holy Spirit, if I will respond to it I can have the marvellous joy of doing what I was destined to do; doing what God himself wrote into the code of my life. This is for every child of God, in the same way that DNA is for every human being. We cannot be a human being without having DNA. We cannot be a child of God without a spiritual DNA written into our beings by a loving God.

Changing the analogy, there is written into us, as it were, a computer program of destiny, a program which includes individual works prepared beforehand for us to walk in.

Here, then, we face our first dilemma! Most of us know, or at least hope, that God has a special plan, or purpose, for our destiny and for our lives – but how do we discover it and fulfil it? One thing is certain – God is not a fatalist. These works, and this destiny, will not just unfold – it will require our active participation and co-operation.

Someone once described eternal life as 'finding the will of God and doing it now'. God wants our lives resonating with purpose and Divine activity. He wants to develop in us a consuming desire to be in step with His overall purpose and the many individual works that He has prepared beforehand for us to walk in. He wants us to see, believe and act upon the truth of our importance, our meaning and our relevance. We are important enough for Him to write His own computer program of destiny, with pre-programmed works and pre-ordained days. A 'spiritual DNA', with all my spiritual genetic codes intricately woven in. And that is for everyone reading this book!

The big question is, how do I seek it, find it, discover it? The answer, in fact, is lovely and easy. It begins with the primary command of Jesus – Seek first the Kingdom of God. We have heard this taught for years. We all know it is a primary command and yet with all this emphasis, I know from talking to different people, that many, if not **most**, of us are vague in our ability to implement that message or genuinely apply it to ourselves. In most cases, it is not out of disobedience, but rather a lack of knowing exactly what it means. We want to do it – but *how?* It's like the proverbial bar of slippery soap – every time we think we have grabbed it, it shoots out of our hands. It must also be obvious to us that our destiny and the Kingdom of God are inseparably linked.

Having talked with thousands of Christians over the last twenty years, it is clear to me that there are two things which Christians invariably find it hard to do. They are, firstly, to know the will of God and, secondly, to find the Kingdom of

God. We want to follow Jesus and we want to be obedient, but we can't understand how to make the Kingdom of God relevant in our own lives. We know we should look for it, but we don't know where!

The question is – has Jesus given us the address? Our friends, Phillip and Joanna had a new house. We knew it existed, we knew they had purchased it, we had seen pictures of it and heard people talk about it – but we couldn't find it because we didn't have the address! We drove round their village for ages looking blindly for the place. That's how it is for many of us – we search for the Kingdom, we have some Bible pictures of it, others have talked about it, but we seem to wander round and round wishing we could find it. It's like looking for buried treasure by digging up any and every bit of soil that we come across. It takes years, even decades, to do it, and we only find it if we are lucky!! And yet all the time we have a map in our possession, which gives us the precise location and tells us how to unearth it.

Jesus tells us where and how to find the Kingdom. He says that people will not say 'here it is' or 'there it is', because the Kingdom of God is – where? *Within you (or among you)*! We don't find it, because we are looking 'out there' instead of starting 'in here'.

For years, maybe even decades, we have looked 'out there' – in the Church, Kingdom houses, Kingdom principles, Kingdom businesses, and of course there is no such thing!! Of course we won't find it if that is where are looking. Jesus says the treasure of the Kingdom is so easy to find – I have put it *inside you, or among you.*

As we will discover together, when we were born into the Kingdom of God and baptized, or filled, with the life-source (the Holy Spirit), God imparted, or awakened, in each of us a number of spiritual gifts. There are at least twenty-seven of them recorded. It is certain and beyond doubt that each one of us has one or more, and most have several.That unique blend of spiritual gifts that you and I have, has been given to us as a deposit of the Kingdom of God. The dynamic of the Kingdom of God, its power, its energy source and its force is the Holy Spirit. Spiritual gifts within us are one of God's primary connections through us into our sphere – our world. THE KINGDOM OF GOD IS WITHIN US!

As we seek, and discover, the unique blend of gifts that has been given to us, as we lay down our lives to steward them, we will discern our unique destiny. We will also find that our ongoing search for the Kingdom of God is directed, almost as if we have some kind of autopilot, and when we have found it we go from horizon to horizon with increasing expectancy.

This is a releasing truth. As we find the deposit of the Kingdom within us or amongst us, and as we put that to work, the Kingdom of God will continually open up before us.

As we seek God for the gifts, we find that our spiritual DNA – our spiritual genetics, our Divine computer program – is encapsulated in these gifts within us, supernaturally planted by God himself. As we seek and begin to use them, the coded will of God begins to emerge, becomes understood and becomes a reality. The stressful habit of constantly looking for God's ultimate will becomes reversed. We find the seeds of God's will in the gifts He has placed within us. As we use them more and more, the water of God's Spirit causes the harvest of His purpose to naturally grow from the seeds of His gifting.

People have often asked me the question, 'How do I discover my destiny in God?' Much is made of one passage in Philippians, which says, 'I press on to take hold of **that** for which Christ Jesus took hold of me.' I have met thousands of people from different cultures and different generations who are longing to find *that* – the one thing that God has apparently called them to. This weekend Carleen, our eldest, had a powerful encounter at an event called 'Ultimate Intentions', when God again endorsed for her a specific calling to nursing and Africa. I have no doubt that God has spoken, and Gill and I are absolutely delighted. But it is not like that for everyone and I don't think it should be. In fact we run a real danger of bringing disillusionment to the many, whilst releasing and enthusing the few.

Sigma

For years there had been a certain restlessness in me, constantly looking for the *'that'* to which God has called me. Every time there was a significant appeal to turn life and possessions over to God, Gill and I would stand at the front. In fact, on one occasion, we even stood in the offering bowl out of a sense of desperation to find the elusive *'that'*!

We have had some significant prophetic words about other nations, which we have prayed over and assessed to be of God. We have had certain promises from God which are still to be fulfilled. So, in one sense, you could argue that we were justified in our search. During one season of particular restlessness, I had a dream – a very simple dream and one which was also very memorable. I saw just one still frame, standing out in three-dimensional form, and it was the Greek letter 'sigma' or 'Σ'. God-given dreams are both wonderful and frustrating at the same time. Of course it drives you to God to get some understanding. I tried calling my theologian pal, Mike Beaumont, in Oxford. 'Mike, what does the Greek letter "sigma" mean?' He went away for a few minutes, looked it up in his special theologian-type books and said, 'Sorry, David, it doesn't mean anything more than capital "M" in the Greek language.' 'Thanks pal!' I thought, 'Theologians – who needs them?!' Then he added, 'But it does have some mathematical significance, although I don't know what it is.' They're a great help, these Bible teachers, aren't they!

Later that day, friends of ours, Dave and Elaine Crick were taking Gill and myself out to the theatre. I was telling them about the dream and about Mike's comments. Dave said, 'Let's ring my son Andrew and ask him what "sigma" means.' Andrew's answer was straightforward. 'It means the "sum of things" or the "sum of everything" in an equation.' As soon as he said that, I remembered the symbol in the Excel spreadsheet on the PC. The penny began to drop. When I was praying about this a little later, I sensed God saying, 'You are looking for one thing, one single *'that'*. But son, your destiny is the sum total of everything you are doing. The destiny is in the sum, not in one individual part.' I felt as if a huge weight had lifted off my shoulders. I felt released and I felt strangely at peace.

So, for some of us, it may be that our destiny is a single *'that'*. Probably for the majority of us, it will be the sequence of small things that, in total, make up our destiny, the sum of many things we are doing with God and for God. If that is the case, how do we enter into it?

Entering in

That, I believe, is fairly simple. Our general calling or destiny is determined by the spiritual DNA which God has put into us. The belief that God has written His spiritual DNA into us should have already affirmed to us that God's gifts and His calling in our lives are inseparable.

A person's general call is equivalent to his or her gift mixture. God does not give us gifts which He does not call the recipient to use, nor does He call someone to do something for Him without equipping them with the necessary gift or gifts to do it.

Besides the general calling, there will also be a specific calling or what we sometimes call our 'ministry'. This describes the particular way in which we exercise the gifts, or the setting in which we exercise the gifts.

People who are looking for the call of God need to find the gifts of God within themselves. As they faithfully and consistently put them to work, their calling becomes opened up and out.

It is as if God has given us local currency to invest into the Kingdom of God. In fact, in the parable of the talents, that is exactly what the word 'talent' means. It is an economic unit – it does not refer in any way to ability. We could say that it is as if the 'ecu' of the Kingdom is the unique combination of the spiritual and natural gifts given to us. As we lay down our lives to steward them, and put them to work, our destiny unfolds in front of us with ever-increasing wonder and with ever-expanding horizons.

Prophetic at work

For example, my primary gifting is prophetic, both in the sense of 1 Corinthians chapter 14 and also, to whatever small degree, Ephesians chapter 4. I am sure, from twenty years of working this out, that I am equally as prophetic in the working world as I am in churches around the world. The prophetic model has many variations in scripture, but I am sure you can think with me of some of the more obvious ones.

1 Chronicles talks about the prophet bringing practical solutions for success. In today's language you might call that 'strategy'. In my working arena, I run seminars around the world on practical business principles for success. Today, for instance, I have been talking to Suresh Punjabi, who runs Corporate Communications in London, and who has been asking my company for marketing advice and hands-on help for plans to grow his company in a defined pattern. All that is an extension of being prophetic.

Prophets have dreams. Jacob, for instance, had a dream about genetic ramifications in his herds of goats. I remember travelling for one client, running seminars around the UK. At the end of the seminar, delegates were asked to sign a standing-order for my client's service. At venue after venue, delegates were not signing. I knew the service inside-out and knew its integrity and its value. There was no conflict in my mind about its value or about the appropriateness of asking for the standing-order. I asked a few intercessors to pray. That night, or rather early the following morning, in my bedroom at the Hilton Hotel in Garforth, Leeds, I had a dream or a vision. In the dream, I saw two pages of paper with typed sentences. I woke up, quickly wrote down what I had seen and asked the conference manager, Janet Turnbull, to type them up and put them on an overhead. I used the overheads in my presentation, and something like 60% of the companies signed up that morning! When they had all left, I sank to my knees in the Harewood Suite and praised God for His faithfulness.

Late last year, Gill and I were staying at a ranch in Sturgis, Michigan where we were working with Glen Middleton and the Church there. The huge ranch was property belonging to a Christian. He was a poor man. One night God woke him up and gave him strange numbers that kept running through his head. He tried to sleep but was disturbed by the number pattern that kept flashing through his mind. Shortly afterwards in an act of faith he secured a patent on those numbers believing that God had shown him them for a reason. In due course it transpired that these numbers were a formula for a type of acrylic. The man made millions when NASA used his pattern for plastics aboard the Apollo. There is a factory in Sturgis that uses the formula today.

Prophets call out for integrity and righteousness. One of my favourite clients is Nick Robinson, the chairman of the Marketing Guild. Whenever he introduces me, he introduces me as the 'Company Conscience'. I treasure that title more than any other I have been given or have taken! In one issue of the Guild's superb newsletter, there was an article which I felt was inappropriate. Nick disagreed with my judgement but nonetheless printed an apology and gave my point of view. I appreciated that approach.

Prophetic people preach or communicate in a way which builds up or motivates. I do that in church settings around the world and also in business settings around the world. Prophetic people are responsible for equipping people for works of service, which invariably involves helping people to discover who they are and what gifting they have. Gill and I have travelled to a number of cities running seminars on spiritual gifts – helping church people discover who they are in

God. In the business world, clients will ask me to help identify staff skills and aptitudes. This is the prophetic in action in both spheres.

I have been writing this chapter at the coast today, to get some peace and seclusion. Tonight I travel back to Basingstoke for a church-based meeting with John Denning and Bryn Franklin, to encourage, challenge and equip all the prophetic people from our church. All these things – the wonderful variety and mix, the seamless flow between work and church – are part of expressing the gifts and ministry which God has placed in my hand. This is the prophetic at work.

Teaching at work

I know countless scores of men and women who have a teaching gift. The state school system is a place where Christians with gifting and vision can really make a difference, and many do. One of my friends, David Robotham, has been a teacher in the state sector – in fact he was a very successful headmaster. He has also run two schools on the African continent. Let me quote from his written school philosophy from the International School of South Africa:

> The school is a Christian foundation . . . Most important is the contention that our Christianity governs our relationships. Self-sacrificing love is its foundation, and mutual respect for cultures, religions and people of different backgrounds is its outcome. We therefore welcome and encourage students from non-Christian backgrounds, and provide for them to attend worship and to receive instruction in their own faith. Our Christianity governs our curriculum. The Bible speaks of God Himself sustaining the creation by 'knowledge, understanding and wisdom'. We want our students to be knowledgeable, for ignorance leaves them open to manipulation and creeping incompetence. To acquire learning is merely 'to think the thoughts of God after Him'. (Kepler)

This small extract is another illustration of God-implanted gifting expressing itself outside the Church and in the heart of the educational establishment.

I have a real and ongoing passion to see a whole new generation of teachers who will find God's voice, and then bring His voice back into our state-run schools. I believe it is a particular emphasis of God's right now. There is a need to support the faithful men and women who have stuck it out through some colossal changes, but there is also a need for a whole new generation of visionary younger men and women who can be part of God's new wave into education.

Pastor and mercy giver

Margaret Veitch expresses both these giftings in the hospice at Basingstoke, which provides an incredible level of terminal care. Pain relief, palliative care for other forms of distress and suffering, personal love and unstinting devotion are all part of Margaret's daily job. When she is home, she and her husband, Charles, run a pastoral team and provide pastoral care for the Chineham church.

Joanna Thompson, some twelve years ago, asked God what he wanted this 'little housewife', as she calls herself, to do. Today, she has an overseeing role with over one hundred Pregnancy Crisis Centres in the UK. Her first one, in Basingstoke, now sees over one thousand women each year. Many babies have been saved, and some mums who have been born again are now rooted in the Church. Recently, Joanna was involved on prime-time TV, in a show about the right of teenagers to have children. She speaks in Europe, South Africa and, a few months ago, found herself speaking to MP's in Sweden!

Leadership

What about my friend Chris Lever? He works as a consultant with the consulting organisation known as Teleios, which is staffed by Christians. Let me quote how he expresses his gift of leadership at a very high level in the corporate world. He writes, 'Our passion is to see people making breakthroughs, as leader, manager, employee, as teams, as the Board, and as the shop-floor production group'.

Teleios is retained as the 'preferred supplier' to many leading international corporations like the international computer giant IBM, as well as to smaller groups such as Little Havens Children's Hospice. Various books and published articles use their work and several of the team work for Cranfield University and Business School, probably the leading school of its kind in Europe.

Leadership also includes local, national and international government. This area is now receiving attention in the West – out of 650 MP's in the House of Commons, up to 120 meet for prayer. Not all of these will be born again, but it's a start! In a recent issue of Ethos, the prime minister and foreign minister of Norway were interviewed, each with a strong Christian faith robustly expressed.

Stewardship

I heard of a man called John Smith in British Columbia, Canada, who was depressed over the rape of the forests. Someone faced him with this question as he was about to give up – 'Whose trees are these?'

He went back to his forestry with renewed vigour and insti-gated a programme called the 'Silver Culture Programme', where he blended harvest with re-plant, and discovered a whole new method of logging Silver Spruce which saved the trees. That programme now runs through the whole of British Columbia.

I have only been able to highlight a few examples, but there are countless ways in which our gifts, ministries and natural talents can be expressed with joy, with anointing and with faith into the world of work. These examples are a tiny proportion of what can be done by stewarding our gifts and talents. As we do that on the shop floor, in school, on the wards, in the fire engines, behind desks, in hotel conference rooms, let's remember we are in partnership with an infinitely creative God and let's look to him to anoint our life, our gifts and our natural abilities. If we are not in a job where these things can be done, let's ask God what we should do and where we should go.

If you have some examples of gifts and ministries at work, then please e-mail us at *insightmarketing@btinternet.com* and we may be able to include your story in any future editions. Alternatively mail us at Insight Marketing, Cricket Corner, Lynch Hill Park, Whitchurch, Hants, RG24 7NF.

Chapter 14

THREE HOMOSEXUALS AND A LADY CALLED MARGARET THATCHER

The music is pumping its sensual rhythm. Staff from my clients' companies are already dancing on the floor. I am sitting at a crowded table waiting for my first course. A very drunk man is sitting on my left and straight ahead is a Danish lady, whom I shall call Maria. I am sitting there and, in the deafening racket of that darkened room, with a boring conversation about marketing going on next to me, I am crying out to God to speak or to do something. I have already been approached by three homosexuals wanting a bit of a cuddle. Yuck! And then the moment that I have come to love begins. God begins to speak to me about the lady opposite, about the tears she has cried for one of her children, about how pleased He is with her care of her child and how He understands her pain.

With a fair bit of nervousness, I begin to relate all this to her. She begins to cry and says, 'I can't do this! I can't do this!' 'Can't do what?' I ask. 'I cannot cry,' she replies. 'They call me Margaret Thatcher at work because I am the hard one. They must not see me cry.' Maria dashes off to the ladies and returns with her face freshly powdered. While she is gone, God begins to show me some specific things about her son, how she could understand him, how she could do certain things to bring him up and what his background means for the future. She starts to

140

cry again and disappears to the restroom for the second time. I talk to her for a little while and offer to pray for her son. She grabs at the offer and takes our home address so that she can call or e-mail if there are any new developments.

I love those moments. I always feel inadequate, I usually doubt what I sense God is saying, but they are nearly always powerfully productive. And there is always this wonderful sense of being in harness with the power of God at work.

In harness with the power of God at work

Of all the issues covered in this book, this one probably vexes me the most. So far we have talked about a number of ways in which the power of God and the anointing of God moves in all kinds of different facets of working life. But, ultimately, God's business, whatever it is, will always be about people and I long to see more of the power of God at work touching people.

We have counselled, taught or worked with thousands of people over the last decade or so. Throughout that time it has been rare to see real evidence of a powerful dynamic demonstration of God in a work setting. I keep asking where the men and women are, who will truly see in practice the second half of Ezekiel chapter 47. The river reaches the sea, there are places for many nets, there is a multitude of fish, everything lives, there is healing – why? Because the river is there. I don't believe that passage belongs to the millennium only. There are, apparently, well in excess of 400 million Spirit-filled believers. If not our generation, then whose? Please tell me!

Acts says, 'but you shall receive power when the Holy Spirit has come upon you – and you shall be witnesses to me . . .' The Greek, as most of us know by now, is 'dunamis'. If, as a genera-tion, we have received the dynamic, the dynamo, the dynamite – where is it at work? Is it leaking somehow, or are we in some way disconnected? Maybe there are some principles which can focus our mind on this issue –

1. An unshakeable belief that I am called of God to my job

Why is this important?

i. More than half our waking hours are usually spent here. The balance of our time is divided between family, church and other ministry.

ii. Many people have doubts about their calling and therefore never have a whole heart! (If our minds or activities are filled with church-based, so-called spiritual activity, then we will have a divided heart.) I have already alluded to the fact that there are good business people who won't hire Christians because they know that the person's heart is not with them!!! Christians don't always make the best employees because of particular religious attitudes which rob the employer of the heart. Fundamental to being in harness with the power of God is having a whole-hearted attitude.

iii. With the appointing comes the anointing! If God has called me here, if this is His choice of function for me, I can expect His power to be available. So, preliminary to harnessing the power of God, is settling this issue. Some people are confused by the lack of some supernatural, powerful, Divine encounter but the Bible makes it clear that this, in fact, is the norm. If I take this seriously and ask God to make my appointing at work crystal clear He will speak, and when I have settled the issue that this job is His appointment for me, I will experience His anointing if I reach for it in faith.

2. Being clear on my root motives in my job

Jesus expressed it as, 'Seek first the Kingdom of God and all these things shall be added unto you'. In work, our daily motive should be that God has called me here and this is where I will interface, or introduce, the Kingdom of God into a time/space segment! We have looked at this in some detail in chapter six – the issue needs to be resolved.

3. Having expectation

We could say here 'according to your faith be it done to you'. If we know we are called of God and if our motives are pure, then we can legitimately expect God to move, and our faith and expectation levels can grow. I have been shocked at the number of people over the years who do not believe in the power of the Spirit in their workplace. I would like to suggest some basic expectations. God Himself is with me at the desk, on the machine, on the campus, in the surgery, in the air, on the sea. If we could really grasp His imminence – the reality of His presence – daily, intimately, genuinely, it would help us to be harnessed to His power. I don't know where you think He is on Monday morning? I can tell you. He is in your office. He is brooding over that hospital ward. In fact, as both Joshua and the writer to the Hebrews experienced, God's view is, 'Never will I leave you, never will I forsake you, so we can say with confidence the Lord is my helper . . .'

Can we grasp that, please? '*Never*' means never! '*Never*' includes the office argument, the dying patient, the occult colleagues, the board room confrontation, the mundane assembly line, the NATO base in the Balkan conflict. '*Never*' means never!

4. Being in harness requires sowing before reaping

Harnessing the power of God in my life requires sowing before reaping. It begins on one level – with us, not God.

Will I sow my seed for this life, this day, this family, this year, this house, this career, this business – or can I find a way to sow my life into things that have lasting and permanent value?

Sowing of seed is a picture used right through the scriptures. Jesus used the concept for one of His most famous parables, or stories. Sowing of seed would be a poignant, powerful picture because everyday people were well aware that their future depended on enough seed being sown in the right place and at the right time.

What we are in God next week, next year and next decade will depend on what we sow today. The power of God in my job – in your job – depends on what we sow.

What does it mean to sow?

When we sow seeds in our garden we take the seed, pop it under-ground (depending on the weather, we may water it or we may not), sometimes we even forget about it, but we expect that the life of God in it will cause it to grow in its proper time and produce beauty, shape, food, or whatever it's supposed to produce.

When we sow the seed of our life, we do it in four basic ways –

1. We sow with our mind – what we allow our thoughts to do.
2. We sow with our activity – what we do with our time.
3. We sow with our words – what we say.
4. We sow with our resources – our money, homes, posses-sions . . .

To summarise – sowing is what we do with our minds, our words, our activity and our resources (what we put ourselves and our possessions into). Sowing gives us the correct per-spective – that God's power does not normally produce mirac-ulous or spectacular harvests overnight. Normally it takes time! What sometimes happens is that we pray into an area and lose heart because of apparent delays. We're impatient!

Some practical applications

1. Doing good.

'Let us not become weary of doing good . . .' (that is, doing pos-itive, Spirit-led, sacrificial things). It can be easy to give up. '. . .

For at the proper time *we will reap a harvest if we do not give up.*'

My friend, Vic Gledhill, calls this 'acts of kindness'. His Church and their related groups have been living this out for some years and a good number of people have been converted to Christianity in the process.

I remember queuing in the canteen at Technicon. There were three or four Christians in the line. A lady was walking back to her table and slipped with her tray, spilling food and shattered glass all over the floor. One of the Christians, without even thinking, cleared up the mess. The lady was overcome by the kindness and it opened up several ongoing conversations. It also made an impact on a Mormon employee, who later brought his whole family into the church, was converted and finally baptised. 'Therefore as we have opportunity let us do good to all people especially to those who belong to the family of believers.'

Salt softens, cleans, heals, stings, purifies and preserves. Light is a model, or an example, shows the way and is an embodiment of truth – a voice.

There is a famous saying, '*when the going gets tough, the tough get going.*' How about, '*when the going gets tough, the tough get **sowing**'*?

2. Recognising the needs around us

Julian Sayer from KBC writes:

When I began working in the computer industry, it was very easy, at times, to kid myself that those around me were in little need of help. The external appearance was one of sophistication, confidence and determination to succeed. It wasn't long before my 'awe' of these 'beings' wore off.

Over the years, I have had the opportunity to talk with, and pray for, people facing issues such as divorce, cancer in the family, a friend in a coma, office back-stabbing, psychological problems and abortion.

Each of these people have approached me, wanting to talk and knowing that I was a Christian. God will often use a natural friendship that has developed at work. However, some of these people have been those who I would not naturally have spent time with outside the office environment and others have been those whom I have not considered to be good at their jobs! The point I am making is that God will often break down barriers we have created in order to reach someone. Very often, God will reveal the root of their attitude problem which, if dealt with, benefits the company as well! There have been many times when I have been quick to judge people, only for God to correct my attitude by bringing about an opportunity to serve them or pray for them!

3. Loving and serving our neighbour

Recognising that there are well-concealed needs amongst those we work with is not enough. As I have mentioned, people will come to us on occasions, but this does not mean that we should sit back and wait, in the hope that a queue will soon form at our desk!

Jesus consistently took the initiative. He went to people, He asked questions, and He died for us without an invitation. He really loved people and we need to really love people too.

I can recall a number of occasions over the years where I, with others, have prayed for 'compassion for the lost', thinking that this is a gift from God. Nowhere in the Bible are we told to request this 'gift', but we are told many times to 'be' salt and light and to love our neighbour.

'Compassion is learned, not prayed for!' (Vic Gledhill)

Giving without expecting to receive is contrary to the attitude we see around us, especially in the world of business. It is all too easy to allow wrong motives to creep in and we must be careful to discern between opportunities to serve and opportunities to communicate the gospel verbally.

4. Love in action

Examples of loving and serving opportunities, that are within the capabilities of most of us, are as follows:

- A 'thank you' note
- An apology for an inappropriate remark
- A word of encouragement
- Cards on special occasions
- Information spotted on someone's hobby
- Buying someone's sandwiches for them
- Taking an interest in people's families
- Making the tea for the team/department

Lorraine had worked for the team for over two years. Most of the team were Christians although most of the company, including Lorraine, were not!

She was on a low wage (certainly compared to the rest of us) and struggled to make it stretch each month, especially as she liked to party! One morning, she called the office to say she wouldn't be in as her car had broken down yet again. Before she knew what was happening, two of us appeared on her doorstep, took her to work and delivered her car to a garage and by 5.30pm they were re-united.

Lorraine was close to tears as she suddenly realised that each member of the team had demonstrated their love for her by contributing to having her car repaired. This one act spoke more to her than anything we had said previously when we were sharing our faith with her.

As far as I know, she has not yet given her life to Christ, but that is God's call. I truly pray that the next time Lorraine encounters a Christian, she will take a step closer to making that decision.

People can ignore almost every direct communication of the gospel, but they cannot ignore us loving them! John sums this up with the simple but effective encouragement, 'Dear children, let us not love with words or tongue but with actions and in truth.'

5. *Praying*

I was running a marketing seminar in the Hilton Hotel in Basingstoke, for the Marketing Guild. As is my normal custom,

I was shaking hands with delegates before the start and asking what they were looking for in particular. I had nearly finished the fifty or so delegates, when I came to one of the last, sitting right in the front close to my lectern. I said to him, 'What are you hoping to gain from today – why have you come?' He replied, 'I have come today to discover my destiny.' I was more than a bit surprised, so I said the first thing that entered my mind – food! I said, 'How about we talk over a snack at lunch?' 'Fine,' he said.

Lunchtime came, the delegates left and this man and I were left alone in the room. He began to tell me that he had a broken marriage, he had been in the occult and so on. I shared about salvation, I shared about deliverance from the powers of darkness and I asked him if he would like to have both now. 'No, thanks,' he said. 'Bother,' I thought, 'this is what usually happens to me – I wish my mate Gary Gibbs were here – he would get this guy saved.' Then I asked him the only other thing I could think of: 'Would you like me to pray for you?' 'I would really like that,' he said. 'What would you like me to me to pray for?' I asked. 'I would like you to pray that I would discover my destiny,' he said. Looking round to make sure there was no one watching (I was in my best suit and I am a bit homophobic!), I laid my hand on his shoulder and began to pray.

A tear or two formed in his eyes as the presence of God began to manifest itself. 'That was wonderful,' he said. 'Would you pray again?' 'Sure,' I said. 'What shall I pray this time?' 'Please pray that God would make Himself real to me.' This time the tear or two were in my own eyes.

He didn't give his life to God there and then, but he did very definitely experience the tangible presence of God, and I was able to put him in contact with a Christian businessman in his locality.

Chris Lever faxed me this story today –

After a long training day, a delegate came up to us and said, 'There is something different about you lot in the training team.

You are Christians, right?' I must confess that, at that point in the day, I was not in the mood to respond in a Christian-like manner. Both my colleague and myself had given our all during the day and our batteries were low. Faced with the abrupt challenge, my brain was already rehearsing a defensive reply, when the person broke down and explained that she had once been a Christian but had lost her faith. She told us her story which was marred by pain and betrayal, and then asked us to pray for her. What a pleasure! That evening she returned to her spiritual home.

What is fascinating about both these stories is that neither Chris nor I were trying to witness. We were not wearing fishes or crosses. God was at work and fortunately, on these two occasions at least, we didn't spoil it for Him!

6. *Just Being*

This is a story from Phillip Denning – a salesman:

With each appointment that I go to, I make a point of always spending a few minutes in prayer beforehand, praying specifically for the person that I am visiting. I pray simply that, whatever the outcome is business-wise, I will in some way be a blessing to the individual and to their company, and that in some way, no matter how small, they will be better off for having met me.

Over the last few years, God has given me numerous opportunities to share the Gospel with non-Christians, and to have fellowship with and encourage Christians also in the business world. Some of the times that stick most in my memory are as follows:

Just over two years ago, I met with an engineer who had showed an interest in our company. We got on well, despite the fact that he was probably the crudest man that I have ever met! After about six months, he decided to place some business with me, and informed me that the reason that he knew we were 'kosher' was because he had seen my Bible in my car!

Until that point I hadn't even mentioned to him that I was a Christian.

A year later, I was visiting another company local to him, and I really felt that the Holy Spirit was prompting me to call in and see him again. However, as I was in a rush, and didn't want to get held up, I didn't go. Later in the day, he rang me out of the blue! 'I am ringing to say "Goodbye,"' he told me. He then went on to say how his business was going under and how his wife had found out about the string of affairs that he had been having and had tried to kill him on two occasions by stabbing him! He had now decided to end his life, and was ringing me in a last attempt to find some hope, as he had remembered that I was a Christian. Thank God that he did. That was six months ago, he is still alive and he is regularly meeting with his local vicar!

Another time, I was in a meeting, again with an engineer, and after a few minutes it became clear that we were to trying to evangelise each other! As we chatted, it came up in conversation that his wife had suffered for nearly twenty years from M.E. to such an extent that she was completely wheelchair bound.

About three months later, I met him at a seminar, where he promptly ran up to me crying, 'She's been healed!' It turned out that after hearing about a church in North London where miracles were happening, he had taken his wife along. The pastor there simply laid his hands on her and she instantly got out of her wheelchair and has been fine ever since. As he left the seminar, he called out to me across a packed room, 'Isn't it great to follow a God who still heals the sick!'

Shortly after this, I heard about a young lad in my own church who had this same horrible illness. I called my friend and got the details of the Church in question. The young lad is now healed!

Recently, I was selling to an engineer in South Wales. Amongst other things, I chatted about a recent trip to India where I had been working alongside several Christians in a church out there. At the time, the engineer was reluctant to buy because of scepticism over the product I was selling. As I related some of my stories from India, he informed me that he was now convinced to buy, as no Christian would deliberately seek to rip him off!

7. Dreams and prophecies

For those non-charismatic readers amongst you, this section may make your eyes roll into the back of their sockets – sorry! For the rest this will be significant! The Bible is full of dreams, visions and prophetic words. Jean-Paul Jackson commented on the fact that Polycarp, Tertullian, Justyn Martyr, Origen, Jerome and Gregory all had dreams and the creed came through a dream. Someone calculated that nearly half of scripture is related in some way or other to the fulfilment of dreams.

In Joel and in Acts, we are told that dreams will be a regular feature in the last days when the Spirit of God is poured out on all flesh. Presumably 'all flesh' means charismatic and non-charismatic. A lot of the dreams in scripture came to working men or women. The same is true of prophecy, which also features in the last days and also appears in the same two passages with regularity. Now, of course, there are dangers in this realm, but the dangers must not frighten us away from the very real power and positive direction that these two dimensions of God's power can release for us.

Timothy was pretty level headed – a bit timid, perhaps, but he certainly had the destiny of God written into his life and he also had a fairly significant spiritual dad in Paul. In other words, probably more than most of us, he could be pretty clear and confident about his future, wouldn't you think? Read what Paul says to him, 'Timothy, my son, I give you this instruction in keeping with the prophecies once made about you, so that by following them you may fight the good fight, holding on to faith and a good conscience. Some have rejected these and so have shipwrecked their faith.' 1 Timothy v18–19 NIV.

There is some fairly controversial stuff there, isn't there? 'Do you follow the prophecies? Some have rejected these and shipwrecked their faith!' Of course, the balance to all this is given elsewhere, where we are instructed to weigh any prophecy and hold on to what is good. Not all dreams are from God and not all prophecies are from God. But when they are, the injunction is clear – *follow them*. In other words, they are His instruction and His direction, and they are very definitely part of being harnessed to the power of God.

In an earlier chapter, I recounted a dream which had a dramatic effect on a business strategy. In another very short dream some six or seven years back, I dreamed of a Swedish businessman offering me a new business to start up. I jotted it down in my prayer journal without thinking too much about it. Two years later, Gill and I were seeking God for the way forward. A number of possibilities had dried up and we sensed God poising us for change. During this time a Swedish businessman telephoned me and offered me a new business start-up. I wasn't sure, and in praying about it I flipped through my prayer journal. I came across this little dream again. It gave me the confirmation that this was God's provision. Today that business turns over £3million and employs upwards of sixty employees. I am grateful for that dream. There were dreams involved in the starting of this book, which gave confirmation and instruction. I am grateful for those dreams.

A young working woman with a prophetic gifting recently sent me this story:

I had a dream where I saw a young girl in a white room being attacked by a multitude of people. She was desperately trying to escape. I became aware that I had 'the key' to unlock her situation. As I took the key and unlocked something, she fled into another white room, a place of indescribable peace.

The following day I approached this girl, who was a very close friend of mine, and shared the dream with her. After talking for a few hours, she shared with me how she had been through an abortion. She had never been able to share it with anyone else. Through the experience, she was able to get some Christian counselling and after much pain is now in a place of peace.

Chapter 15

A STONE'S THROW

Lac Leman

The hotel 'Le Beau Rivage' is situated in one of the most breathtakingly beautiful Alpine areas of the world. I had been conducting a marketing review there for a Swedish company, and in the process I became very close friends with Kiell Tofters and his wife Gertrude. Kiell was the marketing director and, in the first meeting, our mutual faith had emerged and caused a strong bond to develop. At the end of the day together, Kiell, Gertrude, a consultant friend of mine – Kees Rosies – and I stood in the moonlight overlooking the beautiful lake Leman, and on its shores we began to pray. We prayed about Sweden, about destiny and about what God might have in mind for our newly formed friendships.

Ten years later, I had the privilege of praying for elders to be inducted at the church where Kiell is now the senior pastor. During these ten years God has answered the prayers of that night in some powerful ways. That contact led to the founding of my own business. It opened up a relationship between us which led to ongoing visits to Kiell's church. It has facilitated the exchange of prophetic dreams and prophetic direction both to individuals and churches. And, in the process, Kiell has been able to reach out to hundreds of other leaders in the Swedish church, encouraging and strengthening them. That's the power of prayer and a simple example of one expression of it in a working environment. Of all the essential ingredients for work, prayer at work has to be at the heart. It has, countless times, been the key that opened or closed situations in my own experience.

Disciples of prayer at work

Isaac Newton said, 'All my discoveries have been made in answer to prayer.'

Prayer is one of the most underrated, under-marketed, under-explored elements in the life of Christians at work today. Our approach to it individually, and as a church, can be so stereotyped, so predictable and so utterly unimaginative. If we approached marriage with the same lack of freshness and creativity, we would be, of all people, the most dull and lifeless.

When marriages go wrong, sex or money are often triggers, but the final rot and decay sets in when real, open and honest communication breaks down. Exactly the same is true of disciples who lose their faith in Jesus or who backslide. Tithing and Bible study are often the first reflections of something going wrong as both fall by the wayside – but you know it's deadly serious when communication with God falls down, and prayer stops. For that reason amongst others, the enemy targets prayer as much, if not more than, any other single area. That is so true for the world of work.

If we are truly going to be disciples of Jesus, then we need to understand His thinking, we need to understand His methods and we need to know what was important to Him and why it was important. In short, we need to find Him and follow Him!

The New Testament resonates with prayer. There are more references to prayer than there are to 'basilea' – The Kingdom of God – two more, to be precise! 163 versus 161. We know we're commanded to 'seek first the Kingdom', and yet of equal weight are the examples and injunctive to pray. We can't find the Kingdom of God without prayer.

For the Master Himself, prayer was central. The fact is that prayer preceded all He did and prayer followed all He did.

Jesus needed prayer and so do his disciples at work

Jesus did not pray out of obligation or obedience – He prayed because it was natural to Him and He prayed because He loved the process of communication with His Father more than anything else. He knew that His own spiritual resources were measured or limited. They have an end – they are not infinite. Jesus knew when virtue – spiritual power or spiritual resource – had gone out of Him and He also knew it emptied. It was something that needed topping up, needed to be replaced. Too often we assume something that Jesus never assumed. We can assume that we have the grace and strength to handle what God gives us to handle – and we cannot!

Just because God opens doors of work opportunity or ministry, or both, we cannot assume that we have some automatically turned-on power source which will enable us to fulfil what God has drawn down from heaven. Everything God gives us to do is intended to be done in genuine partnership with the Holy Spirit. That partnership can only be activated, or realised, by the process of prayer.

Someone once asked Dwight Moody, the famous evangelist, 'Have you been filled with the Holy Spirit?' 'Yes,' he replied, 'but I leak!' We need to believe this and understand its relevance and it will help us substantially to become disciples capable of living daily in victory. When we give out relationally or spiritually at work, we don't automatically get topped up – we need to go back to prayer for God's refill and we forget it at our peril.

An air-conditioner needs to be constantly topped up with water, but the reservoir is usually hidden. Because it's hidden, you can't always easily tell that it's empty. It will run for a while, start to give out unwanted heat and then finally burn out. It can so often be like that for working men and women. If anyone on this planet could have managed without prayer, it was Jesus himself – sinless Son of God – and yet Jesus makes it clear time after time that He was unable to do anything in His own authority. In John's gospel, Jesus says, 'I speak just what the Father has taught me', 'I stand with the Father who sent me', 'These words you hear are not my own, they belong to the Father who sent me', 'He can only do what He sees the Father doing', 'By myself I can do nothing. I judge only as I hear'.

How did Jesus *see* what the Father was doing, how did He *hear* what the Father was saying, how did He *know* when the Father was sending Him, how did he get *taught* by the Father? – the answer is prayer. It was in the process of prayer that Jesus drew His vision, His healing, His understanding and His certainty about timing. Surely we kid ourselves if we think we can find it anywhere else. How many of you would like to find Jesus? – then discover where He is!

In Proverbs, we discover that God invented 'hide and seek' – He loves the game! 'It's the glory of God to hide . . . it is the glory of kings to search . . .' When our kids were young, we used to love playing hide and seek. I remember one of the kids saying, 'I'll go and hide and if you can't find me, I'll be in the airing cupboard.' The disciples and the crowds regularly hunted and searched for Jesus, like some Divine game of hide and seek. The funny thing was, they nearly always found Him in the same place. He still plays the game and I can tell you where to find Him – I know where He hides! Would you like to know where He hides? I'll tell you! The crowds and the disciples found Him – *in the place of prayer.*

Nothing has changed. You and I can find Jesus in exactly the same place – the place of prayer. Jesus Christ, the same yesterday, today and forever. The disciples found Him in the place of prayer then, and that is where we will find Him today.

He ever liveth to make intercession! If that is where He always lives, then that is where we will always find Him! Augustus Strong said, 'The impulse to prayer within our hearts is evidence that Christ is urging our claims in Heaven.' J. Elliot said, 'God is still on the throne, we are still on His footstool and there is only a knee's distance between them!' If we want to know what the Father says in the machine shop, in the school, in the office, on the ward or in our software department, then we will find that in the place of prayer.

An approach to prayer for disciples to follow

Are there any clues from the life of Jesus which can help us with prayer? The answer is – yes, loads! One of the most helpful is a model which Jesus gave, in Matthew's gospel, which enables us to pray by God-given topics and which give us a powerful framework for an hour's worth of prayer at a time. First, let us look at some terms used in the gospels which give us video-clips of Jesus at prayer – twenty-three still frames from the gospels. Before I share them, let me ask you to visualise your own prayer times. Close your eyes and think about where you pray. Where are you? What is going on around you? What sights and sounds are impacting you?

I wonder what your answer was. My guess is that most of you saw images of your lounge or dining room, your office or kitchen. There is one common problem with every one of those places. Can you guess what it is? In a word, distractions. Invariably there are jobs crying out to be done, people wanting your time, carpets to Hoover or last night's dishes to wash.

If Jesus were standing in front of you now, and you asked Him the same question, I think I know exactly what words would come to his mind. Let's try it. 'Jesus, what images fill your mind when you think about your prayer times on earth?' The following is a list of the answers He has already given to that question –

Images of Jesus at prayer

Often
Withdrew
Secret
Shut the door of your room
Lonely places and prayed
Went out
To a mountainside
Spent the night praying to God
Facial appearance changed
As usual
Reaching the place
He said 'pray'
Privately
Solitary place
On a mountainside
By himself to pray
When evening came
Alone
Very early in the morning
While it was still dark
Got up
Left house
Went off to solitary place

I am touched – moved – when I read these descriptions. I wonder what images filled your mind as we read them together. I find it so fascinating that it doesn't tell us much about *what* He said, but describes in detail *when, where*, and *how*. This is a great study for us to do at home, but let me pick on a few areas.

He got away, right away. He *withdrew* – that is an active choice, a discipline, for disciples in a busy world. He had to get away privately to a solitary place. He had to be alone, He had to be 'by Himself to pray'. He found lonely places. When did I last withdraw? When did you last find a lonely place to pray privately? The funny thing is, if you are not used to it, you may find some difficulties at first, like fear of the open, of animals, of aloneness or busyness trying to crowd in.

And one of the first lessons you learn is to overcome these things by prayer!!

Very early in the morning, while it was still dark, he *got up* and left the house. Again Jesus is choosing times when there is no-one else around. He leaves the house, with its job lists, its busyness and its people, and He is off on His prayer-walk.

Jesus walked and prayed. Ron Trudinger, one of my closest mentors for years, drummed the 'walk and pray' concept into me. I find it so helpful. I am a fairly active, even hyperactive, individual, so it helps me settle my soul and plug in – it gets me motoring. I have one friend who walks seven miles most days, and prays as he goes, and his answers over the years have been quite amazing. Walking and praying can be a sensible option for people in their working environment. It's one way to get some prayer in without raising problems in the process.

Back to Jesus. He gets up in the morning, He gets up in the dark and He goes at sunset in the cool of the evening. He did it *often*. It says 'as usual'. This was His normal practice, not unusual or abnormal, but usual. 'On reaching **the place**' – there was one special place, in a garden or on a mountain. That one place was so special, that He faced all the horrors of the cross in the familiar, reassuring sweetness of that usual place!

When we lived in Basingstoke, I had a place – a special place – where I was at home with God. I can remember most of the times I was there very clearly, and it was a place where I saw what the Father was doing and heard what He was saying (It was a small area known as Bedlam Bottom). In Whitchurch, where we now live, I have a fabulous place over-looking Watership Down – it is my 'usual' place, my lonely place.

Several times, He was recorded as praying on the mountain-side. A couple of times a year I go into the Pennines, and when I am there one of the things I love to do is to walk into the hills.

Every time I have done it, Jesus has met me. I was there recently with two leaders and I took them to a spot I love. As we stood there, just out for a walk, the Spirit of God came and one of the brothers began to weep as God met him. I cannot forget my outdoor prayer experiences. They are memorable, as Jesus has always met me. Where did God meet Moses? On the mountain. Where did God meet the seventy elders? At the top of the mountain.

A Stone's throw

In the hour of His greatest anguish, Jesus went to the one place where he knew He could meet with his Father. This is how Mark describes it: 'Jesus went out as usual to the Mount of Olives, . . . He withdrew **about a stone's throw** beyond them and knelt down . . .'

Nearly all Jesus' prayer was solitary, in lonely places, at quiet times, on mountains. For the average Christian, most of our prayer takes place in stuffy homes, sitting down, feeling drowsy and constricted. If we are going to be disciples, let us follow Him into the open, into the lonely places, into the private, into the 'usual place' – our spiritual spot!

The 'usual place' gets associated with prayer and, in the open, God's creation – His playground – frees our mind, lifts our spirits and primes our hearts, our souls and our minds for prayer. Joshua and Joel have created a small area at the furthest point of our garden, about a stone's throw from the house, where we can go and be alone have a fire or walk around. Some of this book was written down there. The beauty of 'the stone's throw' is that it is just far enough to be near your closest friends still, but far enough away to be out of earshot and distractions!

Intercessors on the move

I'm a great believer in intercessors praying specifically for people at work. Gill and I consider ourselves very blessed to have three couples who have committed themselves to pray for us. I have asked each of them to contribute some aspect of their experiences –

John and Barbara Moore write:

Safety, success, sanctity, serenity . . . and sanity! These would summarise our prayers for Dave and his family in every area of life! Proverbs 22:9 says, 'He who has a generous eye will be blessed, for he gives bread to the poor.' Proverbs (the book for the working person) also says in chapter 11:25, 'The generous soul will be made rich, and he who waters will also be watered himself.'

John and I have been called to intercession and the above verses, mentioning being generous, giving, watering others and so on, we feel are descriptions of prayer life.

Early in October 1991, John had emergency major heart surgery, but went into a coma and was dying from complications. I was also ill, which meant we were homeless, because our home was tied to the job which I could no longer do. In November, John started his recovery but we were both in great physical and emotional need. God has provided us with a home in Basingstoke, and it was here that our relationship with Dave and Gill began and subsequently started us off praying for them, for their work as well as home and ministry. We soon learnt that 'secular' work and 'ministry' are the same (as Jewish folk have always maintained). **Both** are holy. We could have done with that knowledge when **we** worked in Bristol and Oxford!

We also began to see that intercession was a gift which some are particularly graced for, and this re-fuelled John's ongoing unseen ministry of prayer. His health situation means that he has the very precious commodity of **time** so we 'beg' Dave and others for updated prayer request sheets, as John gets frustrated trying to work without one. Whenever he is hospitalised, John takes them with him, however ill he is. 'I've been given a new life and I don't want to waste it', is his theme. I also use the prayer list but I am at my happiest and best in 'crisis' praying, and love to fight in prayer. My Christian nickname is 'Battling Barbara'!

The phone rings, someone says 'Please pray!', I stop what I am doing and respond. Like Eleazar who went to bed with his sword still stuck to his hand, so I like to carry on until I know I'm through on the issue! Apart from praying for Dave at our church celebrations and 'River of Life' meetings, we also pray for him whilst he's abroad on work trips as well as ministry ones. We also pray for him to 'find work' and find time to get everything done that is pressing on him. We also have the privilege of praying this book into being, and anything that God plans to result from it.

We are both retired Senior Citizens and are glad to do this work. For us there is no retiring in the Kingdom of God – only refiring!

We pray for other folk too, but we would love to have more feedback. We want to celebrate when our prayers are successful, or keep praying when things aren't yet happening! Whilst the Holy Spirit **can** and **does** prompt us to pray without having natural 'knowledge', we would appreciate being able to spend time fellowshipping informally with those we are committed to pray for – we want to know how they tick, and we want to share their joys and their sorrows a little more.

As well as running a very valuable marketing services company, David Crick has a real call to intercession. He says,

The practice of obedient prayer has opened up the whole business we are now in. During 1996, God called me three times to set aside half a day of prayer and fasting. Twice I lost the discipline, but the third time I obeyed and have by and large kept to it. It is no coincidence that, during February 97, the business started growing with a continuous stream of the 'right' people and the right kind of business. We have grown from a turnover of £86,000 to £400,000 plus in two years. We have scores of answers to prayer in the business world. Let me leave you with this one:

We were running seminars in Tampa, Florida, and part of the seminar involved me in generating enquiries in a live broadcast telephone demonstration. We were working with a local construction company. I got chatting with the M.D. and it transpired that his son was struggling with severe alcoholism and was, as his dad put it, a prodigal. I asked him if I could take on his son with a commitment to intercede for him. Imagine our joy when, some months later, we received a letter confirming that his son had come back to the Lord. As he said in his letter, 'My son . . . continues to do great; a continuous answered prayer. I have lived the Prodigal Son and it is wonderful'.

I remember waking up one Saturday morning feeling great. On the Sunday I was due to fly out to Helsinki with David Crick to run a marketing seminar in Helsinki. David's role was to do a live telephone demonstration, amplified to the entire Finnish audience. I remember standing in our garden, the sun shining with unusual warmth, the trees showing some sign of blossom, when the phone rang. It was David Crick. 'Dave, my passport has expired, we have tried the Post Office, the passport office and everyone we can think of but I cannot get one.' My calm Saturday was gone, the engine of restless anxiety started to fire into life and began to rev. I thought of all the money spent on the promotion. I thought of our professional appearance and I thought of a few other things besides! I did what I have done so many times and called the intercessors – in this case, Chris and Ros.

This is what they subsequently told me:

We felt almost immediately that God was in this and that the passport, despite all of the human effort, would not be issued in time. We felt that another man, less experienced, was the right one for the occasion. On the Monday, the day of the seminar, we prayed that they would get good business deals and bookings for more seminars, but that they would be God-given and not due to the slickness of the presentation – it would be in spite of the circumstances. We prayed that the Father would show Dave His grace and mercy and that the work would come from His hands – 'His strength made perfect in weakness.'

In fact what happened was exactly that. I took another consultant, Owen Lamb, who had never done anything like this in a public demonstration before. We had a superb time – in fact the Spirit of God came down on Owen and I before the event, and gave us a prophetic burden to pray for Europe, which was a very memorable experience in its own right. Owen did brilliantly. And, yes, I already have one more seminar in the pipeline.

Gill and I thank God for intercessors and thank God for His kindness in giving us three who will often pray for us. This is the season for those in church leadership to encourage church intercessors to find their place for church and non-church activity. This is the time for those at work, whatever our job, to be praying ourselves, but also to be seeking out prayer partners and to offer to be partners in prayer.

I asked Peter Sayer, a retired headmaster, if he would travel with me one day and give me the benefit of his years of experience. I had asked him to share with me the secrets of how he coped with his highly stressful and demanding responsibilities. He gave me a number of practical answers, but his real secret weapon was an elderly lady called Eileen Rowe. Eileen was in her late seventies at the time, but any time he had a major confrontation with the unions, or a difficult relationship with teachers, he would visit her and share with her in total confidence. She would commit herself to pray it through, and he would then feed back the results. Peter reckoned this was his number one key in handling the seriously difficult situations which he encountered.

Let's get a stone's throw away from our work to meet with Jesus, so that we can carry His life into our work. And let's find the intercessors who know their gifting and enlist the willing into prayer service.

Chapter 16

DISCIPLING MEN AND WOMEN IN THE WORLD OF WORK

Picnic at Aldermaston

This was not one of the best days of my life. I had been running some businesses for the church. We had set up one of the largest Christian bookshops in the country and we were also running a publishing house and a growing printing press. At the time we were exploring the role of church in business and we very quickly discovered the practical and biblical wisdom that the Church can govern ministry, but it cannot biblically operate a business. I had contributed to the discussion and the decision, but it was painful. The printing press was sold to another company, and as part of the arrangement I was going with it!

Today was my first day at the new venture and I was feeling very low. The feeling of leaving the church's employ was a bit shattering and the future was one big 'unknown' ahead of me. Brian Rebbettes was my new boss, and he and his wife took me out for a picnic lunch at the Aldermaston woods close by. As we sat there that first day, chatting away, their loving act coupled with an encouraging card from Gill my wife began to give me hope, and more than that, it began to posture me towards something new.

What followed in the subsequent years were some of the most formative experiences in my life. Brian began to disciple me at work. He looked for ways to open doors of function for me and ways to sharpen my selling skills. He shared his office with me so that I could listen to him on the phone. We could congratulate each other on successes and discuss the failures. He was the first and only man to really confront me on my love of money. He challenged me in my marriage and encouraged me with my children. We would share scriptures and revelation together, and we often prayed together.

He put his money and support into ideas that I created and actually participated in those new ideas himself. When he sensed I had something worthwhile to say, he would actually find church groups for me to share with. He and his wife Anne taught Gill and I to have weekends away, and their generosity made them possible. Here was a man who called me up to be what God had made me to be. Here was a man who lived the Kingdom of God at work. Here was a man who served God in his business, who loved God and loved his staff and who, in the process, discipled many of them. When Brian ultimately sold his business and we both moved on to different things, I actually felt bereaved and the feeling of loss was with me for many years afterwards. What an example, what a privilege to be mentored in that way and what a responsibility to live up to!

The problem is I am not in that league. I have a go here and there, and it really is just a go. I suspect many of you feel the same way.

Discipling at work

I was prostrate on the carpet of my hotel room, with my client crying out to God from the very depths of his being. This was not the first time I had experienced the heavy weight of God's presence forcing me to my knees, but it was the first time it had happened in a coaching session with a client. God was there and the coaching session that day included the sharing of scriptures, deep personal prayer and some practical suggestions for family, as well as business, situations. What had happened? I am not really sure, but I am aware, from this example and others, that the climate is changing. The working world is desperate for practical solutions to life dilemmas, not just work dilemmas. The training world today freely uses the term 'mentoring' and 'coaching'. It is not even rare – it is common and accepted practice. The chances are, if you are a nurse or a teacher, a manager or a lathe operator, you have already experienced mentoring or coaching.

In the last twenty years or so, thousands of you reading this book have been trained and discipled in your churches, and you carry a treasure that God may well want you to deposit into other men and women, Christian and non-Christian alike, if you could be open. If you will allow me some prophetic licence, I do believe God is actually opening up a season where this will become increasingly commonplace and you may find you have two talents, or even four talents, ready to invest into others.

Gerry was a non-Christian who worked for one of my UK clients. 'David,' he said. 'Would you consider mentoring me? I don't know what it means, but I would really appreciate it.' My response was, 'Let me think about it.' When I had reflected, I came back and this is what I said, 'Gerry, you know my faith. If I mentor you, it will be inevitable that I weave my faith into the experience, because that is who I am, and it is an integral part of my own development.' Gerry didn't hesitate. 'I expected that,' he said. 'Shall we go for it?'

We had some wonderful times, usually an extended lunchtime with my client's blessing, once a month. Each month, I gave Gerry an assignment. The last one was to find ten things that he could learn from in the life of Jesus and His leadership. When we met next, we had some pressing business and my intention was to leave it for the next month. I could sense that somehow this was really important to Gerry. He was almost insistent that we discuss it. Gerry began to read the ten things. He got to point three or four and he started to shake, he found it hard to get the words out. What were those words? Let me quote them for you, 'Come unto me all you who are weary and heavy laden and I will give you rest. Take my yoke upon you and learn of me, for my yoke is easy and my burden is light.'

What was going on? It's simple – Gerry had been asking some questions of me in the mentoring process, and he was getting his answer direct from God's word and with the powerful impact of the Holy Spirit. Those words answered some questions for Gerry and, amongst other things, enabled him to see that a change of role was a desirable next step. Gerry has moved on but we keep in contact, and in fact he called me last week and we have arranged to meet up shortly. We are also trying to find an appropriate *Alpha* course for him to go on.

I had a client in the USA – someone I respect highly and who in fact has mentored me over the years without realizing it. He asked me to quote for coaching one of his senior sales staff. When we had agreed the contract, he said, 'David, I believe this concept is good, but there is going to be real value in you giving some of your personal mentoring or discipling into this man, and that is what I am really excited about.'

I relate these two examples because it is not my natural 'forte'. I don't offer coaching or mentoring in my business arena. I am not even particularly good at discipling in the Church world. I mention these examples because, if God can do it through me, He can surely do it – and probably better – through any reader of this book. I suppose I would love to provoke and challenge you – you almost certainly have more under the bonnet than you realise. Could it be that there are people in your office, your shop-floor, your ward, your practice or among your clients, who have been asking for mentoring without using the word? Could it be with a bit of prayer and alertness you could be 'God's answer with skin on' to a colleague, a peer or even a manager. Who knows?

Let me give another example from my friends at Teleios. Chris Lever writes:

Over a four year period we have been working with a European Headquarters group of senior managers. We had become close to them, with the relationship shifting from consultant to trusted friend. A corporate buyout had suddenly left them without jobs.

What had once been a team full of sparkle, energy and a 'can do' mentality was quickly reduced to a group without hope. Individuals had put their life and their very soul into building their part of the business. For many it had cost them a lot, but they had paid the price because they figured what they were trying to create was worth it. What took years to build was suddenly disassembled overnight. As they faced the future, with questions like, 'So, what has the last ten years been about?' 'Have I got what it takes to go on?' 'Do I have the courage to start something new?' 'I didn't realize I would feel like this – who can I trust now?' we shared a few tears, because we shared their pain. You see, we had walked with them on their journey. We told our story, one which has seen great blessing and great pain too. We shared the dilemmas that we had faced and we shared our hope.

Together, we explored in depth their hopes and fears and where confidence was located. Over some months we saw a shift in thinking, attitude and desire. Hope had begun to return. We had the tremendous privilege of hearing and exploring people's dreams and of standing with them as each made hard choices. We served them as best we could.

A year on, we are thrilled to see many of the 'half-baked' ideas we had shared together being realized. As many of our friends found a fresh vision for their lives, they began to achieve the extraordinary. Now trading in their own companies across the world, they are committed to working in a different way from before. They say, of Teleios, that we inspired their dreams. I think all we did was to listen, to care and to breathe some hope into weary souls. That is not the end of the story, as we still walk with these good friends and we still share their hopes and dreams. Who knows where the journey will end? Perhaps at the cross, and that would be the start of another adventure!

For such a time as this

Our fractured world and our work colleagues, with their fractured relationships and fractured dreams, need mending. Could it be that 'for such a time as this' God has placed you in your workplace? For some of you reading this, it may be that God will talk to you about getting prepared for 'such a time'. If that is the case, how about a year or two at Bible college? 'What!' I hear you cry. 'Surely that's for full-time Christian workers?' Yes, full-time Christian workers in the work place, that's exactly what it's for! The quotes in this book from Julian Sayer and Chris Bawtree, for instance, are from men who have given up a year to go and get a thorough grounding in the Word of God. Some colleges offer specific modules relating to the Kingdom of God and work (King's Bible College and London Bible College amongst them).

Or at least take your own growth and development seriously. One of my colleagues, Andrew Kenward, wrote in this context:

> When I reached the age of forty, I realized how little I knew about both business and my faith. For example, could I explain 'justification' or 'the Second Coming' easily to an unbeliever? What did I really believe? As a result, I embarked on a course of learning, in all aspects of my life. I found that I had a new hunger for information. I used to read very little – I still don't read enough – however I now have a systematic program of reading. There are always several unread books ready on my bookshelf. I listen to tapes when I travel rather than listening to the radio or music. I find that tapes are an easy way to absorb information and fit in well with my busy lifestyle. In general, I take every opportunity to develop, learn and ultimately change.
>
> I would like to revisit those years again and apply the skills that I have now acquired through training, reading, listening to others and having a more mature approach to sales – and see what difference I could make. I believe that it would be considerable.

I do believe that the world is ready for many of you readers. 'Go therefore and make disciples.' How about it?

Chapter 17

RADICAL REPACKAGING AND STUCK CHURCHES (OR CHRISTIAN LEADERS GET BACK TO WORK!)

At least the chapter heading got your attention! Folks, this chapter is going to rattle cages and set cats amongst the pigeons. If I am wrong, may God forgive me – if I am only partly right, we could see one of the biggest releases so far in 'stuck' leadership teams, whether they be 'New Church' or traditional.

The sacred cow

Whilst visiting numerous church groups, I have the privilege of meeting quite often with different church leadership groups, elders and so on. It is quite common to see 'stuck' churches. By that, I mean godly men and women on church staff but with a fairly pedestrian church growth, a fairly pedestrian level of life and a certain local, parochial, even introspective, pre-occupation. It has been extremely rare, in my twenty or so years of visiting churches, to see elders or ministries leaving church staff and going out to work in the real world. I find that quite strange – I really do. There is almost a panic alert when the possibility is mooted. At the same time, there are thousands of young men and women looking for room to express their fledgling leadership and their fledging ministries but, with great health care and an 80% policy of dead man's shoes, little hope for them to be involved in any meaningful way. The Levites moved aside at fifty years old, probably for this very reason – to make room for the thirty-year olds with their fresh vision, fresh faith and fresh vitality.

The sacred cow, I suspect, is 'once on church staff, always on church staff – once an elder, always an elder'. Paul never had a calling to full-time ministry. Paul never had a call to church staff. His call was as an apostle to the Gentiles. If that meant manufacturing with other workers for a season, fine. If it meant setting up a team to do that while he lectured at the local school, fine. But there was never an assumption that he was full-time church staff. We don't know with the same clarity what the specific call for Priscilla and Aquilla was, but we do know they ran a business, we do know they used their business resources for the work of the gospel and we do know, by inference, that the calling was not to full-time church staff. In fact, the phrase 'full-time' does occur once in scripture. There, that's got you alert now! It actually refers to a non-Christian in a government role!

Now for the jugular! Dear Christian leader, can I question your calling, without shouts of 'Heresy!' or waves of panic? If 'full-time' is not a Biblical term, how come in your testimony you say, 'I felt called to full-time ministry'? I don't doubt for one moment that God called you, but I do question the interpretation of the unbiblical phrase 'full-time'. When God called you, did He actually mean a salaried position on some church staff?

For some He did, for others I wonder. Did he actually say, or even remotely infer, that this church staff position would be eventually with a pension and would be until retiring age?

Or is it possible that he called you to a ministry that might just be more powerful if you had a job or a business which you ran? You talk about discipleship, but could it be that business, with ten, twenty or a hundred people, could provide the most incredible outlet for your anointing and your gifting? Is it possible that the faith edge we had when we pioneered new churches, twenty years back, has shrivelled because we are church staff? At one level, some don't have to live by faith financially in the same way.

Maybe if you ran a business or had a job, that faith edge would come surging back and the yeast of faith and life might just start to ferment again in your local church or stream. Maybe for some it is time to go back to work literally. Maybe for others it is time to have a year at work, or a day a week at work. Maybe it is time for some to destroy the sacred cow and grind its form to dust. Maybe it is time for some older brothers and sisters to consider how they might make room for the 'twenty-some-things' bursting with spiritual fertility and energy.

Maybe it is time for all of us to revisit our calling – that super-natural encounter and to ask God, without fear, what it means in the light of understanding about full-time and church staff. Imagine the excitement if He said to you, 'Go and start a business, go and work in that school or go and nurse on that ward'. Wouldn't it be exciting to have to exercise faith at a different level? Wouldn't it be fantastic to have all that contact with non-Christians? Imagine how many others in your church or congregation would be called up, seriously involved, because you weren't available to do it all. Imagine what it might do for church finance – it might release £10,000 or £50,000 a year for aggressive, effective evangelism, or third world mission, or whatever. Imagine what that might do!

Like many of you reading this book, I have had my 'calling'. I was working in Tanzania with YWAM at twenty years old. I came down with an inner ear infection, first in one ear and then in the other. The infection was acute and left me at times deliri-ous. All through that time, I prayed and cried out to God in one of those desperate seasons that many of you will identify with. The only direction, the only verse, that God revealed during the whole of that forty day period was this, 'He that has an ear to hear, let him hear what the Spirit says to the Church.' I didn't understand it, as I had not encountered prophecy much at that point, but I knew, in the depths of my being, that God had spoken. At the end of the forty days, I travelled down to Harare, in Zimbabwe (Salisbury, as it then was). Again I came down with some rather violent sickness. It was diagnosed by one doctor as malaria and dysentery. The hospital, however, could find no trace of either in my blood sample. Two kind, elderly ladies looked after me and, whilst I was recovering, I walked into the study of their bungalow and there on the floor was a book. The book was open at a page which had this verse at the top, 'He that has an ear to hear, let him hear what the Spirit says to the Church.'

These two encounters have always remained with me as my calling into the prophetic ministry. I don't kid myself – I am not a Paul Cain or a Jean-Paul Jackson, but God has called me to hear what the Spirit is saying to the Church to some degree or other. I didn't know what those verses meant until years later. I did however assume that my calling was 'full-time', 'church staff' – call it what you will. But I was so wrong. It has been liberating to work on the cutting edge of consultancy, to travel the world and see a seamless blend between the prophetic in the working world and the church world. And it has been so fulfilling to have God expose me to things, and speak to me in ways, that on church staff would simply not have happened.

Let me share the story of a new friend who has come to the same conclusion from a very different vantage point and for very different reasons. His name is Andrew Sercombe, he lives in the south of England, and this is what he writes:

Radical Repackaging

I will never forget the trauma of leaving the 'full-time Christian ministry'. I fulfilled all the negatives described on every psychometric test I've ever done. Pain, rejection, betrayal, disappointment and a whole lot more indescribable reactions swept over me, threatening to drown my shredded self-confidence for ever. The eighty-member village church, which we had started from scratch fifteen years previously, became a source for me of the deepest sadness. My decision to resign prevented further damage to me, to the family and to the innocent majority in the congregation who had little or no idea of what was going on.

Looking back on that time towards the end of 1995, I can now see more clearly what was happening. The focus of my own vision had changed. I had become frustrated and disillusioned with the 'status quo', and I found myself in conflict with a handful of sincere, well-meaning people in our Community Church who wanted to keep things as they had been. I simply couldn't do that.

So I was out, discovering a new world that seemed every bit as intimidating, challenging and seducing as that of the earliest explorers of America. A verse from the Bible became very important to me at that time. God was telling the Old Testament prophet Isaiah that he would make him 'a light to the nations'. I knew I could trust Him to make me a 'light' to people in this different context. I felt quite strongly that I wanted to use the knowledge and experience I had gained in my past two careers – teaching Design and Technology for ten years and pastoring a church – to serve the business world. I wrote out a Personal Mission Statement. It was a defining moment.

Naïve? You bet! It slowly dawned on me just **how** naïve I really was. I felt as if I had innocently bitten off far more than I could chew. This was an entirely different way of life! I had to learn, and change to, an entirely new language full of abbreviations, initials and business jargon I didn't understand. (I remember with embarrassment someone having to explain to me what a USP was!) And I had to learn a substantially different culture. Having to market myself and charge for my time were major mountains to climb and utterly foreign to my past, where a person talking positively about what he or she can contribute was seen as suspicious, even as proud and arrogant, and would certainly be refused. I had to change my lifestyle, my clothes, my car and even my watch! A lot of the time I was close to zero; pain and change were everywhere I looked. I had landed alone on a foreign shore. Yet I had to have answers and find where I fitted in. Inside I knew I actually did have those core answers, and would eventually gain the strength, skill and insight to make them real to others.

The first priority was to gain knowledge and understanding

of the culture in this new world. I needed it fast if I was to survive. I couldn't afford university (we were on Family Credit for a year) so I decided to create my own 'university course' by reading the finest and the best of business writers. Stephen Covey, Robert Dilts, Charles Handy, Margaret Waitley, Tom Cannon, David Wheeler, Tom Peters, books on people, business psychology, philosophy, structures, management, communication, NLP, the future – thick ones, thin ones, old ones, new ones, expensive ones – are there cheap ones? – I read 'em! Dozens of volumes purchased, read, marked, learnt and inwardly digested meant I could feel myself changing. I went on every free course I could lay my hands on, and two I had to pay for!

Slowly I managed to get some work. Redundancy workshops, communication skills workshops (I practised these on friends and family), supply teaching, one or two bits of simple 'consultancy', some personal coaching work; it slowly drifted in. I did various practical jobs to keep bread on the table, mending this and fixing that for people. (I remember putting 'flaps' on a huge industrial chicken house containing 7,000 free range chickens. They were inside, I was out in the cold and rain!) Always there was a business development book close at hand. I knew I would eventually have the inner resources I craved.

However what I needed most was self-belief – to know and be confident in who I was, who God had made me to be, and confident with what I had learned over the previous twenty-five years of working with people, not just the last two or three years. Below the surface I was maximising the first-hand experiences I would need for the future, not just learning about running a business, or about handling major change, or about the new order in the global corporate world, or about 'lifetime learning', but experiencing what they really feel like, why they are important and how best to embrace them.

There were little rewards too. Moments of reaping what I had sown. I was surprised when new-found friends clearly valued what I had to offer. I remember a man taking time to phone me in response to an article I'd been asked to write for a business association's newsletter. He said that he would not quit his business after all, but pick himself up and 'get back in there'. That anonymous caller was a real encouragement. I was being a 'light'. As my skills and network of contacts increased, I spent an interesting day with a very astute managing director of a national company. We were looking at the way his personal life was impacting his business culture and vice versa. He was delighted with the day and invited me in to do some work for his organisation. He also paid me what seemed like a huge amount of money for my six hours of wisdom! Apart from that, I knew God was at work.

There are a lot of great people out there! Some helped because they loved us a lot and were just genuine friends. I am sure some people helped me out of pity. Whatever! I needed every last bit of support I could get and I knew it. I was particularly grateful for those high up in the business world who believed in my vision, mentoring and educating me.

It worked! Rock Associates (Personal and Corporate Development) is alive and growing. What I know is being paid for – for considerably more per day than I got as a minister! (A few days ago a client told me I was underselling myself and gave me a cheque for double what I charged him!) People are starting to phone me instead of me phoning them. I no longer have the crippling desperation in my voice. We have managed to keep the house and stay free of major debt. And the call on my life from many years ago to serve God 'full-time' remains utterly valid – **and radically repackaged**.

A caution

I know that this chapter opens up the possibility that some readers will read the material and abuse their leaders with the ideas. May the fear of God be there to prevent that. I know, equally, that what I have written is not for all leaders, but I am convinced that it is for some, maybe even many. If that is the case, may leadership teams reading this *'test everything and hold on to what is good'*. I would actually like to ask every reader to pray right now. Those of you in the working world, would you pray right now and ask God how you could practically help, support and encourage those who are on your church staff?

Those that are leaders, could I ask you now to lay your church-paid status on the altar and ask Him to lead you out into a new dimension of faith, if that is what He wants. If your heart is beating a little faster, if there are one or two tears, if there is that wonderful moment right now where you know He is speaking, then ask Him for a radical repackaging – whatever that means. Go on, I dare you!

Chapter 18

CHAMPAGNE FOR GOD (OR STARTING YOUR OWN BUSINESS)

By definition this chapter will not be relevant to every reader, but equally there may well be hundreds of readers stirred up enough to make this a serious consideration – manual worker or management type.

One of my friends sold his house to Gill and I and then took off for a year with his wife to Bible college in Canada. Why? Well, it became apparent that the training was to prepare him to start his own business. Let Chris Bawtree tell the story in his own words:

How many of us at any time have thought about starting our own business? Judging by conversations I have held with different people through the years, I guess the answer is – many of us. What is it that makes owning our own business such an attractive prospect? Is it the thought of being answerable to no one apart from ourselves? Is it the potential of earning more than we could were we to stay employed? Or is it the desire to be personally ultimately responsible for our income? Whatever it is, the dream to start our own business is often there. However, the reality is that for most of us nothing ever happens. The dream remains just that, a dream.

So what factors were present in my case? Probably all those mentioned above, plus one more, namely that I really believed that owning my own business was ultimately what God had called me to do.

Back in September 1985, I moved with my wife, Jenny, and three of our four children to Vancouver, in British Columbia, Canada to attend a one year course at a Bible school linked to our church. Although I was prepared to be taught everything on the syllabus, my personal motivation for taking a year out was to spend time in God's Word discovering for myself what God has to say on the whole subject of economics. As a qualified Chartered Accountant, I had taken on much of the world's view on the subject and although much of it made very practical sense, I suspected that there were many more principles waiting to be discovered from God's Word. In the course of the year, I discovered much, but by the end of the year, the most important thing God had shown me was the danger of debt. Debt not only made the borrower a slave to the lender, but it also took the place of total trust in God for provision.

Also, whilst at Bible School, I received prophetic words to the effect that I would be the owner of businesses, so armed with these exciting prophetic words, I returned to the UK determined to see the prophecy fulfilled, but equally determined not to resort to borrowing.

On our return to the UK, I was approached by a friend to work for him as the General Manager of his printing business, a position which I accepted gladly and with gratitude. However, within a short period of time, I was experiencing frustrations with the organisation, particularly as the accounts operation was outside my control and the vital information I needed to show me how the business was faring was not forthcoming. After a year or so had elapsed, my friend confidentially told me that he and his partner were contemplating selling the business for a fixed amount and would I be interested in purchasing it? I jumped at the chance. Here was the opportunity I had been waiting for. The prophetic word I had received would now be fulfilled and I would be able to show how a business really should be run. The only problem was that I had no money! But never mind, this had to be God's purpose for me, so we borrowed the deposit and agreed to pay the balance over the next six years out of the profits of the business. After a frustrating year of protracted negotiations and delays, I, together with a colleague of mine, finally purchased the business and we were able to set about putting things right!

At first things were fine, but after a short while, cash flow became very tight and it wasn't long before we were faced with having to make redundancies. This temporarily improved things but then we were faced with our major customer cutting back on his orders, which further strained resources. Another round of redundancies ensued but with the recession of the early nineties really beginning to bite, and under extreme pressure from the bank, the company finally went into receivership in October 1990.

At this point, all my dreams seemed to be shattered. My chance to run my own business had been squandered, I was deeply in debt without the remotest possibility of being able to repay it, and I was facing personal bankruptcy. I felt I had let down my wife, my children, my wider family, my friends and above all, God. What is more, the prophetic word I had been given had been wasted, and it seemed there was no future for me.

But at times like this, one has the choice of either sinking into despair and self pity, or turning to God in repentance and calling on his love and mercy. Thankfully I chose the latter. I sought prayer from our church elders and received much encouragement from them to 'stand still and see the salvation of your God'. I took this as God's word to me and waited on God for his salvation.

Before long, I was asked to do some temporary work with another Christian friend of mine, which subsequently led to an introduction to an insolvency practitioner whose business was expanding rapidly due to the now thoroughly established recession. He was looking for someone to assist him in his business and thought me to be the right man for the job! I realised I had received God's promised salvation and was employed again, earning sufficient income to enable me to pay my way. However, the debts still remained and the need for them to be repaid was weighing heavily on us.

Soon after starting to work for my new employer, I was asked to visit a failing company just prior to its being wound-up in order to prepare some last-minute cash flow projections. These projections confirmed that the company was too deeply in debt to continue. After it had ceased trading, two of its former directors decided to set up in business again, and they contacted me asking if I could assist them with setting up their finances correctly. So I took a half-day's leave, assisted them, sent them a bill and they paid it! Some few weeks later, a friend phoned me to ask if I could recommend a practising accountant who would be able to sort out his annual accounts and tax. Although I was rather out of touch, having been out of professional work for years, the friend persuaded me that I should do the work for him. So I was persuaded and I did eventually do the work. Then another friend approached me, and then another, and it was not long before I realised that God was bringing the clients and work for me. But it took a little longer to recognise that this was possibly the fulfilment of the prophetic word to me.

By now, the work was proving to be quite lucrative and I could see it as the potential means whereby in-roads could be made into my personal debt. So I decided not to spend the earnings on anything apart from debt repayment. The business just simply grew and grew, and over the ensuing years I progressively reduced my time in employment from five days to three days a week. I was also having to work evenings and weekends on my private work in order to meet the demand from my personal clients. Then in April 1997, I took the plunge and became fully self-employed as a practising Chartered Accountant.

Since then the business has gone from strength to strength. The debts have all been repaid and I have never borrowed to support the business. God has always given the increase. Particularly in the early days, whenever it seemed that work was slowing down, my wife and I would ask God to send us more work, and every time we prayed, he answered. Apart from placing a bi-monthly advert in our local church advertiser, we have never undertaken any other form of marketing or advertising.

On many other occasions, I have had clients come, asking me to undertake work for them about which I have had little or no experience. My attitude when confronted with such a situation has always been the same, namely, that I will not reject

what God has brought to me. I am reminded in such circumstances of the scripture which says, 'Make the most of every
opportunity' (Ephesians 5 v 16). Although this verse is usually
thought of by most people as applying to spiritual situations,
I firmly believe that it refers to any situation that God brings
our way. If God initiates the work, he will provide the means
and abilities to ensure it is done properly.

So what have we learned from the whole experience? Firstly
and most importantly, that when God gives us His word it is
folly to go ahead of Him trusting that He will support us regard-
less, and that we should never presume to work out the prophetic word for God, but rather let Him bring it about in His
own good time. Secondly, that when God shows us important
principles from His Word, we should always seek to abide by
them and apply them in the business context.

Soon after the collapse of the company, Jenny and I sought
out the advice of a greatly respected friend and counsellor who
advised me, amongst other things, to write down all the lessons
I had learned out of the experience. I took his advice and I am
so glad I did so, as on many subsequent occasions, I have
extracted the lists from the file and reminded myself of those
lessons so painfully learned. So the third lesson is that we need
to recognise that all of our life experiences have a value. They
can either result in our collapsing under their weight or they can
be used to help us in times ahead. The choice is ours.

Champagne for God

We have already seen that Jesus was the number one example,
from shop-floor worker to self-employed micro-entrepreneur, or
at least a senior partner. I was sitting at an expensive restaurant
in the SAS Hotel at Arlanda Airport, Stockholm, Sweden. We
were eating fish for lunch. I remember that because the fish was
indifferent and I was nervous. My first client had asked me to
type up our contract in English on the hotel's PC, and I had
never operated a PC before. I felt such a Wally! I felt inadequate
and foolish, but I also had this wonderful sense of God's pres-

ence in my weakness. When I got home and shared the news with some friends, we invited some of them round – Derek and June Wickens, and Steve and Margaret Gee – and we had some champagne together. On the floor I had our grey washing-up bowl and a champagne glass. As we thanked God together that night and celebrated our thanksgiving with the champagne, I poured out a full measure into the glass on the floor, lifted it up and then poured it into the grey washing-up bowl. This was my drink offering to God. Like Jacob, who pioneered the idea, God had spoken to me and I wanted to make it clear that, from the very first day it was settled, He had spoken, He had opened the door and the outcome was under His Lordship. It was a very meaningful moment that we shared in that room – a sense of His presence, His pleasure and His commitment to what would later open up. I have never forgotten that day. That was eleven years ago, and, amongst many other small miracles, our business has not yet had one single bad debt! God has surely been in it.

Has God spoken?

The only regret I have is that I did not start my own business earlier. That is one of the reasons why we have encouraged Joel, at eighteen, to start his own business, 'Results in Marketing'. I am so thrilled at the challenges he is facing and the difficulties he is overcoming. If God has stirred you up while you have been reading this book, it may just be that for some it is time to consider starting your own business. The first question is, 'Has God spoken?' There are a variety of ways to determine that. One is in prayer, of course. Often God will give you a sense in prayer and then confirm it with a verse from scripture that jumps off the page and grabs your underlining pen from your pocket.

I think it is quite in order to set some 'faith steps' for yourself. When I started, because I was already on a good salary, our commitments were high, so I asked God for a sign that would earn me some money and which I could service during evenings and weekends. I asked him for a contract that would give me at least some income for the first six months. That is exactly what happened. I had three months' work from a company, which enabled me to buy our first Amstrad PC and put the deposit on a serious car. When I signed my first agreement in Stockholm, it gave us enough income for a year. I had enough faith for that! With Joel it is totally different. He has few outgoings, there is nothing really to lose and so much to gain that he can simply just 'go for it'. I don't know where you will fit on the scale between the two extremes, but you are going to have to settle that yourself, of course.

Share it and wait

When you are sensing God has spoken, share it – not widely, but with one or two trusted friends and with your pastor or leader. Give it some time for faith to rise. Dave Richards is my pastor. I am so grateful for his prayers. I am even more grateful that he has encouraged me to reach out in faith, to keep going when I felt fainthearted and to take risks. In eleven years, I have never had a leader discourage me, and I do feel blessed.

Waiting for God to confirm and settle the issue can be important for the impulsive ones, the faith-filled supercharged ones. But for others, waiting will kill the seed. If you are usually timid, reserved or fearful, don't wait too long otherwise your fear will gobble up your faith and you will rationalise away your delayed decision. When you see the green light, go! The worst that can happen is you lose your house, your car and your Armani suit. You can't take any of that with you anyway, so why worry about it?!

Plan for it

First of all you have to have an idea. What is this business? How do you check that? I have a diagnostic model which I use in training and consultancy it is called FPOOP© Forgive the acronym, but you won't forget it! How does it work?

F stands for fear. What fears does my product or service solve or relieve for people? What fears does it deal with or remove?

P stands for problem. What problem does my product or idea solve?

O stands for opportunity. What opportunity does my product or service create for customers that they couldn't create for themselves?

O stands for obstacle. What obstacle does my product or service remove for customers?

P stands for preference. What preference does my product or service facilitate for my customer? .

If you are crystal clear on all these five, the chances are you have a great idea and you can articulate the good that it is going to do for your customer.

A practical check-list

Paul Davis, FCA, a close friend of mine, has penned the bulk of the following checklist for starting a small business −

What is my motivation?	call of God
	prophetic word
	best way to steward my talents and gifts
	logical development of current activities
	means to an end
What are my core values?	underlying principles
	relationships − internal/external integrity

Have I counted the cost?	money personal commitment responsibility to others and for others
Have I taken advice?	financial strategic, marketing employment
Who is my provider in reality?	God? credit or loans from others? the market place?
Have I thought through risk?	faith what if it fails? what can I manage? what can I insure?
Some key actions	ask God and ask for godly counsel a crystal clear product or service clarity on why people should buy it a total belief in my product or service a plan to follow my key assumptions – checked the critical success factors listed (what must be done and by whom and when) contingency plan set up finance and timing
Key considerations	my own strengths and weaknesses family pressure financial pressure handling success, isolation and failure impact on personal life and church life a business confidant or mentor

These checks are not exhaustive but they will give a starting point. If you can find a business mentor to check these, it would be wise to do so!

Starting later in life and working with your hands

Mike Slydel started his painting and decorating business when he was in his late fifties. He had been made redundant a couple of times and decided to give it a go. Let me pass on some of his advice for any aspiring self-employed tradesman. Mike writes,

Since starting out on my own some five years ago, a lot of things have happened and new experiences have come to me. The proving of God's provision is just one of them. On one occasion, I had just finished painting a house and gone home, when it started to rain. Because time and money had run out on the job, I asked Jesus if He would stop the rain so that it did not ruin the surface of the paint, but it didn't stop. I was really cross to think that I would have to strip off all the paint and start again (For the uninitiated – this is because when it rains on wet paint it leaves little but permanent rings on the finished surface). The next day when I went back there was not a single ring on the paint at all. He had answered my prayer but not in the way I had expected.

Going self-employed is a big thing and needs a lot of thought as there are some big disadvantages such as no unemployment money, sickness income, pensions, holiday pay and, to a certain degree, no security.

Practically speaking there are two ways to go if you are self-employed. You can get your work from big contractors. For this you need to register with the Inland Revenue and produce a photo ID. Alternatively you can set up your own company and deal directly with the public. In this case, having an accountant and a business bank account is a must. This will give you access to the credit world, which in turn will reduce your overheads. Business cheque costs can soon mount up for a self-employed person, so I keep a fairly large amount of petty cash which enables me to buy small items without needing cheques. Having credit is also important for the same reason.

 Insurance is a must for any tradesman, particularly if you work for the construction industry. For a small cost you can register your company name and protect it, if you have a name that is important or effective in the market.

Network marketing as a possibility?

As I shared earlier, I do have some concerns about network marketing especially where it uses church members as its clientele. But there are plenty where that is not the case and where it provides a low-risk, minimal investment way for you to run your own business. It can be a cracking way to start a business with minimum fuss. I was speaking to Bill Cherry of 'Netcom', one of the country's most successful network marketing practitioners. Bill made these comments:

Network marketing enables you to have control over place, type and time. It is self-employment with low-risk start-up. You can start whilst still in another job in some cases. It is a type of work which allows you to practice your beliefs to the full in the work setting. It only works when you help other people make money. You will learn people skills in the process and the fruit and gifts of the Spirit are going to be necessary. This is a unique kind of self-employment where others must succeed if you are to succeed. It is crucial to success that you help others, and mentoring is often a feature of this process.

One feature of networking is that you are encouraged to fill your minds with good, positive, up-building material. The result, according to Bill, is that morals are higher and divorce rate is lower than in other forms of business. In fact I had an e-mail yesterday from someone attending a weekend away at an event with Bill Cherry at Harrogate. One hundred and fifty people gave their lives to God during the Sunday morning worship time!

Has he been speaking?

I would love to encourage some of you readers to ask God if self-employment could be the next step for you. Pray about it, chat to your leaders and carefully go through the steps we have outlined in this chapter. And do let us know if you make it!

Chapter 19

HOW TO EAT THIS ELEPHANT

Adopt the 10% rule

I hope this book has been a motivating, challenging and impacting read. But please don't put it down here. The time you have invested in reading it could transform your life, your church, your family and your destiny.

But of course it never will! It is destined to fail, destined to be a disappointment. Why? Because you won't apply it, will you? Come on now, be honest, you are about to put this book away, aren't you?

You told yourself that you would try to apply some of these principles when you next get a chance. Don't kid yourself! Do something now, and there is a chance that you will make a difference. Leave it, and you never will.

How do you eat this elephant? Easy, the same way you eat any elephant – one bite at a time. Take this material, ask God what needs re-reading, what needs changing and in your prayer diary, or in a chat to a colleague, commit your self to enact that change.

If you are a church leader, would you go to Appendix II and fill in the action form. If you want to fax or e-mail us with your commitment, feel free. If you are in the workplace and you feel challenged to do something in your home church, please read Appendix I and fill in your personal action plan.

Two favours!!

Church leader or working person, would you do me two favours? Thanks −

Favour number one. Write down the 5 key truths or ideas that you know intuitively will give you the greatest change immediately and which God has spoken to you as you have read. Jot them down in the space below.

1..
....

Action:

2..
....

Action:

3..
....

Action:

4..
....

Action:

5..
....

Action:

Please use these at the next possible opportunity. Promise me this. If they work for you, write down the next five and try them.

That is the 10% rule. Take just 10% of the areas you know need to change and focus on them. When you have mastered them, go on to the next 10% and so on. Keep doing it and you will not only read but begin to implement your work as a powerful place of destiny.

God bless you as you put these principles into practice.

Favour number two. Please help us write the next book, or the next edition of this one! Write, fax or preferably e-mail your comment, your testimony or your insight, and if we can we will include it in some way.

email – insightmarketing@btinternet.com

Insight Marketing,
Cricket Corner,
Lynch Hill Park,
Whitchurch,
Hants,
RG28 7NF

Telephone 01256 895529
Fax   01256 895883

WHERE TO NOW? – WORKING MEN AND WOMEN

This appendix was written, virtually in its entirety, by Julian Sayer, a Kings Bible College student, as his assignment:

Integrating the workplace into the Church as a mission field

The purpose of this appendix is to identify ways in which the opportunity and needs of the workplace can begin to be integrated into the Body of Christ and be seen as a mission field well overdue for harvest.

Whilst I would hope that the suggestions given could be applied within any Christian church congregation, any assumptions I make are on the basis of my own experience which has been that of the Charismatic movement.

I would stress that this is very much aimed at those people whom God has clearly challenged to address this whole area and that His direction is paramount. The first sections are intended to provide guidelines for these people, thereby ensuring that a sound foundation is dug and footings laid before the first blocks are set in place.

A good idea or a God idea?

Before you begin to spend any further time on a 'good idea', you had better be sure that it is a 'God idea'. If you believe that God has prompted you to raise this issue within your church, how you handle it will have a major bearing upon how it is accepted.

Share your thoughts with your leader or pastor (the person you look to for spiritual input in your life). They may not see the issue in the same light as you – after all God prompted you, not them, and they may feel the leaders have enough on their plate without extending their boundaries further! Whatever their initial response, ask them to pray for wisdom in the matter over the next week until you meet up again.

Take time out to really study God's word and ask Him for a truly personal understanding of 'the Kingdom of God in the workplace' that is based on sound theology. Prepare your thoughts in such a way that you can clearly articulate the message. Compile a list of all those in your church that, like you, spend most of their waking hours in the workplace.

By now your leader or pastor should have come back to you with what they have from the Lord. For the purposes of this exercise we will assume that you have shared the results of your study with them and you have been encouraged to pursue the matter with the recommendation that you seek God at every stage.

Sharing the vision

> Without counsel, plans go awry, but in the multitude of counsellors they are established. (Proverbs 15:22)

The word you have received will require a major shift in the way many churches operate, and will therefore have to be shared with the elders, for them to prayerfully consider and sanction, prior to delivering to the corporate body. The verse from Proverbs given above encourages us to invite input from others and I would suggest that there are two forums that could be used to test the word, as instructed by Paul

> Do not quench the Spirit. Do not despise prophecies. Test all things; hold fast what is good. (1 Thess 5:19–21)

Housegroup

Have a chat to your housegroup leader. Explain what God has said to you and take him through the theological basis for viewing work as a worthy mission field. Ask him for the opportunity to share your thoughts with the group one evening in order that they can ask questions and pray about the matter. It is important that you introduce your talk correctly by explaining that this has yet to go before the elders and that it should be viewed accordingly.

The benefit of sharing your word with your housegroup is twofold – firstly, you are amongst friends, and in an environment where concerns can hopefully be raised and discussed in a positive manner and your theology challenged, if necessary, without you feeling condemned. The other benefit of sharing in this setting is that housegroups, in my experience, typically consist of a wide cross-section of the community – old, young, mothers, fathers, employed, unemployed, students, singles, couples and widows. Housegroups are a slice of the Church and, as such, an excellent place to understand how the same teaching can be viewed from many perspectives. The views of the older members of the group are especially important and should be sought and considered carefully. Remember, not everyone is going to agree with you – Jesus had the same response – so don't get disheartened, but instead, take on board the comments from the group and make any adjustments that are necessary.

Other people who work

Most people in your church work. The list you have made will confirm this and now is the time to use it! Highlight those people you know well and let them know that you are organising a meeting at your place to talk about issues they face at work. Whilst this is an informal gathering, it is probably wise to inform your church leader of your intentions in order to avoid any misunderstandings at a later stage.

The purpose of this gathering is as follows:

• To share openly challenges at work
• To discuss ways of applying scripture to issues raised
• To share your vision on the Kingdom and the workplace

The turnout will be a good indicator of the general feeling towards 'church and work' and the evening should allow as much time for discussion and prayer (your time to listen) as it does for your time to share. Once again, it is important to acknowledge that you have yet to share this with the elders and that this is still very much 'your vision.' Having said this, there is no reason why this group cannot continue to meet regularly (but not at the expense of housegroup) to discuss issues and share how God has answered prayer.

Taking stock

You should now be in a position to incorporate the feedback you have received from these meetings and people's prayers into your own study material and have a clearer idea of how to present your vision.

Put together a concise summary that can be delivered in fifteen minutes and which provides a clear theological basis for viewing the workplace as an important mission field for your church. Demonstrate how applying Kingdom principles through ethical behaviour and loving your colleagues can extend God's Kingdom where you and so many of the congregation spend so much time. Explain the need for their support and suggest ways that this could be encouraged (some examples are given later).

Before you ask for a slot at the next elders'/leaders' meeting, share your intended material with your pastor/church leader or maybe your housegroup leader. Ask your pastor/church leader to request the slot and ask him to attend with you.

The leaders' meeting

Remember that this is not a board meeting! Your leaders have been appointed by God to serve the Body and they are accountable to Him for their care of His Church. As such they are not expecting a slick presentation (in fact this would probably turn them off) and are seeking to hear God's heart in the matter. God has chosen you to communicate His word so be careful not to add or take anything away from the core message. Remember that some of your audience have possibly never worked in a non church environment or have forgotten what it was like.

Explain how God spoke to you and what He said. Inform them of how you have invited the counsel and prayers of others and that the thoughts you are about to share are based upon this input.

Begin by asking God for His heart to be made clear to those present through what you say and then take them step by step through the results of your study, answering questions as they arise.

Whilst you should gain a fairly good impression of their immediate reaction, it is likely that they will ask for time to hear God on the matter – you've done your bit, it's God's turn now!

Doing the vision

So it's down to me!

You've bided your time and yesterday you were asked to attend the elders' meeting first thing this morning. God has kept his part of the bargain and the elders are cautiously giving their blessing on raising the profile of the workplace as a valid mission field. That's the good news! The only thing is, you're the one who is going to fly the banner!

The elders recognise that for too long the workplace has been ignored and they welcome your desire to apply God's word. However, God chose to speak through **you** and to begin with at least, they want **you** to share your vision across the housegroups with their blessing.

Help! What do I do now?

Pray! God has answered your prayers at every stage and you are accountable to Him over the way you handle His word and His people. Ask Him to show you the most effective way of delivering all that he has given you. Involve the elders in anything that falls outside of the remit they have given and, if time is limited, concentrate on doing a good job of encouraging a small number of groups rather than a poor job with all.

Remember that teaching in many denominations over the last 400 years has largely ignored the importance of God's royal law, 'Love your neighbour as yourself', and allowed a divide between the spiritual and secular to grow and strengthen. Don't be tempted to run ahead of God. He wants to change this as much as you do – the difference is, He knows the bigger picture and His timescales are usually different to ours.

Suggestions to consider

What follows are some suggestions for getting off first-base. They are by no means exhaustive and may well need adapting to suit your particular church.

Pray about each one. Ask God to prompt you if He hasn't already, and talk through the options with your shepherd.

1. Begin with your housegroup

Your housegroup have had time to think about what you have said and may well have some encouraging stories to relate from their encounters at work since you spoke. They will be keen to hear how you got on at the elders' meeting and no doubt pleased to know the result. In short, they will feel a part of this because, having included them early on, you have demonstrated the value you place upon their contribution.

With the permission of the housegroup leader, organise a regular fifteen-minute slot for the next couple of months focusing on work. After that, people may well have become sufficiently conscious of work issues for them to become a more natural part of what they share and what they ask others about.

2. 'Faith at work' group

You might want to call it something else but I would encourage a regular gathering of people who want to apply their faith at work and want to study God's Word and its relevance to their situation. This would be an ideal forum to invite an elder to attend as it will provide them with a good understanding of the issues facing people in today's workplace.

Begin with your original group and ask each person to share during the initial meetings about what their job involves, why they do it, what the environment is like, whether they share their faith, how they approach the tasks, issues they have faced and are facing, etc, etc. Prepare a series of topics to discuss based upon the two key issues of loving your neighbour and Christian ethics which can be the focus for future meetings. Pray regularly for wisdom, boldness and a strengthening of faith as well as for specific issues or topics.

3. Join existing Christian work-related organisations

There are a number of Christian organisations that exist to provide support and contacts for Christians in the workplace. Most of these seem to be aimed at business people rather than traditional blue-collar workers, however my research has been limited on this matter. Those that I have discovered seem to have a good regional set up and hold regular meetings and seminars at which many of the issues facing us at work are tackled head on by people who have put their faith into practice at work and seen God move in marvellous ways.

Organise a group visit to one of these events and follow this up by discussing the teaching over the next couple of meetings. One word of caution. Check out the doctrine of the organisation before you join or turn up – it might just be a front for the Mormons or some such crowd!

4. Take an elder to work!

If your church leaders are to really understand something of the life you live at work they need to go there. If you are a deep-sea diver based on a oil rig in the North Sea, this might not be practical, however most of us work in less remote and dangerous environments and 'the vicar' can usually get a pass into most places even if it has to be at lunchtime or after hours. Ideally you should arrange for them to spend at least half a day with you in order that they can get a good understanding of what you do and what you face. You could even arrange to spend some time at their place of work!

The role of the elders and leaders of the Church is to make sure that it remains a place of strengthening and equipping of the Body for service.

This duty of the elders and leaders can only extend to your workplace if they have at least some understanding of what it entails. (Incidentally, I would recommend that spouses visit each other's workplaces as well! This can really help partners to show an interest in what each other does during their time apart and make a real difference when going through a tough time at work.)

5. Round up the Christians at work!

This is when you nail your colours to the mast and if people didn't think you were weird before, they will now! How you find these people will depend largely upon what your job is and how internal communication is usually handled. You may have a notice board or, more likely these days, e-mail. However you approach this, make sure that if permission is needed it is obtained. A notice or mail that says something like the following should not present any problem to most companies – in fact it might even bless them!

WANTED!

Christians to pray for the company,
for the staff, and for encouragement.

Meeting room 4 at 1pm on Thursdays.

Any questions call Julian on ext 7582
otherwise just turn up

Even if no one turns up make sure *you do* and keep on turning up! Many Christians have kept their faith quiet at work and just turning up to a prayer meeting runs the risk of being noticed by others. Be sensitive to this and respect the major step they have made. Here are some suggestions for prayer during these meetings:

Thank Him for:
- Bringing you together
- Placing each of you in this company
- The freedom you have to meet

Pray for:
- The directors and managers
- Christian values in the business
- Conflicts and politics that exist
- Opportunities to express love to colleagues
- New birth!

- Strength to stand up against unrighteousness
- Support and teaching in your churches
- Specific current issues
- More Christians to join the company

Make sure that you allow time to share concerns and current issues or decisions that are facing members of the group. Just sharing these will help tremendously, and knowing that others are praying for you whilst you are tackling a difficult problem and that God is right with you makes all the difference.

Your meeting is probably limited to an hour, so it may not always be possible to look at specific topics, however try to allocate the last twenty minutes or so to exploring what the Bible has to say on issues such as recruitment, discipline, honouring your boss, etc. Use the material from your 'faith at work' group as a basis for study.

6. Using the Net

Many of us have yet to explore and fully understand the possible uses of this amazing communication tool. Like so many inventions, it has the capacity to do so much good in the right hands but so much evil in the hands of the enemy. One area in which Christians can utilise this tool is as a means of discovering other Christians working nearby. Once you have established contact you could arrange to meet as a group monthly after work for a drink and share what God is doing at work.

The Net is a great way to keep each other updated and request prayer on current issues and job vacancies can be circulated amongst Christian groups.

Project summary

This project is aimed at those people who feel that God has called them to the workplace and to raising its status, from an inconvenient necessity within the Church, to a mission field as much in need of salvation as any other people group. I have tried to apply the principles that I have learned over the years with regard to handling God's word and encouraged the reader to approach their leadership in the right manner. The ideas given are there for inspiration and subject to God's approval before they are embarked upon.

Point to ponder:
We are after all, all full-time!

My personal action plan

STEP 1 .... DATE.............
STEP 2 .... DATE.............
STEP 3 .... DATE.............
STEP 4 .... DATE.............
STEP 5 .... DATE.............

My prayer is ....
....
....
....
....
....
....

WHERE TO NOW?
CHURCH LEADERS AND
LEADERSHIP TEAMS

Congratulations! Thanks for reading this and lasting all the way to the end! You may simply be affirming much of what you already do, but could I encourage you to run your eyes down the checklist and ask the Holy Spirit to show you what changes He would have you make.

What we believe

- Are we clear as a leadership team what we believe about full-time calling, about the worth and value of every job and the need to drop the phrase 'full-time'?
- Have we developed a doctrine of work as godly, work as worship, work as a holy calling?
- Are we agreed that the 'secular/sacred' myth is a heresy, and what steps will we take to communicate that?

What we practice

- Will we re-evaluate the following areas and bring the necessary Spirit-inspired changes?
- Notices – will we change our notices so they read less like a fixture list and more truly represent the world and interest of

our working membership? (Perhaps you could ask church members at work for relevant articles and testimonies.)

Preaching & teaching

- Will we ensure that what is taught is relevant to our working congregations? (a starter list is included in Appendix IV)
- Will we quality-control the teaching so that its real impact is tested for worth and applicability?
- Will we regularly ask working men and women to share the teaching and preaching, so that the Church can learn from the variety that there is in the Body of Christ?

Prayer

- Will we make sure we pray over tithes and offerings with gratitude to God for holy, valuable work and the blessing of money that comes with it?
- Will we try, creatively, to weave work-related issues into any corporate times of prayer and intercession?

Language

- Will we consistently try to avoid using the following terms – 'secular employment', 'full-time ministry', 'sordid money'?

Leadership

- Will we re-consider the way we run leadership team meetings?
- What could we learn from godly professionals in our church?
- Will we plan for every member of the leadership team to routinely spend time with as many working men and women as possible in their workplace?
- Will we offer to serve our working men and women any way we can and ask them how best we could do just that?

Calling

- Will we be willing to face the unthinkable?.
- Are we willing to question, not the calling of God itself, but its assumption of a salaried church-employed position?
- What wise, godly man or woman could I share that with?

My personal action plan

STEP 1 .... DATE..............
STEP 2 .... DATE..............
STEP 3 .... DATE..............
STEP 4 .... DATE..............
STEP 5 .... DATE..............

My prayer is ....
....
....
....
....
....
....

Appendix III

REFERENCES

Chapter 4

Luke 11:51, Mark 6:3, Acts 9:43, Acts 18:18–26, I Corinthians 16:19, Acts 16:14.

Chapter 5

Ephesians 2:10, Psalm 139:13–16.

Chapter 6

1 Chronicles 31:20–21, James 1:7–8, Proverbs 30:18–19, I Thessalonians 5:18, Luke 3:14, Hebrews 13:5, Ephesians 4:2–8, Proverbs 26:10.

Chapter 7

Isaiah 43:1, Genesis 32:28, James 1:2–4, Hebrews 5:8, Hebrews 4:15, Mark 6:3, Proverbs 1:20–23, Revelation 2:26–29, Deuteronomy 28:13, Daniel 6:1–3, Titus 1:5–9, 1 Timothy 3:1–13, 1 Timothy 6:1, 1 Peter 2:12–18, Hebrews 10:38, Romans 4:12, Galatians 5:25, Romans 14:23, Hebrews 11:6, 2 Corinthians 1:24, Romans 10:9.

Chapter 8

Ephesians 1:18, 2:10, 3:8–21, 4:18–23, 5:23–30, Matthew 7:15, 16:16–19, 1 Timothy 3:15, Acts 2:47, 6:12, 14:22–23, 20:21, 20:28.

Chapter 9

1 Corinthians 14:1–28, Ephesians 3:16, Mark 6:3, Exodus 31:3, Ecclesiastes 10:10, Matthew 25:30.

Chapter 11

Proverbs 6:26, Matthew 4:1–11, Hebrews 4:15, 1 Corinthians 10:11–14, Romans 8:1, Galatians 6:1, Matthew 26:4, Proverbs 5:9, Mark 10:6–9, James 5:16, Proverbs 28:13.

Chapter 12

James 5:16, Luke 16:13, Deuteronomy 14:29, 15:10, 16:15, 24:19, 28:1–14, 30:9, Proverbs 11:12, 13:11, 13:21–22, 20:21, 21:17, 21:23, 24:29, Psalm 34:9, 35:27, 37:37, James 4:3, Ecclesiastes 5:19, Luke 14:33, Luke 18:22.

Chapter 13

Psalm 139:13–16, 1 Corinthians 2:9, Luke 17:21, Philippians 3:12, 1 Chronicles 20:20.

Chapter 14

Acts 1:8, 2 Chronicles 31:21, Ecclesiastes 9:10, Colossians 3:23, Matthew 9:29, Romans 12:6, Hebrews 13:5, Galatians 6:9, 1 John 3:18, Acts 2:17–21, Joel 2:28–32, 1 Timothy 1:18–19.

Chapter 15

Proverbs 25:2, Matthew 6, Hebrews 7:25, 1 Samuel 1:15, Psalm 42:4, Psalm 62:8, Philippians 4:6, 1 Thessalonians 5:17.

Chapter 16

Matthew 11:30, 28:19.

Chapter 17

1 Thessalonians 5:21, Romans 13:6, Revelation 2:7.

Appendix IV

BIBLIOGRAPHY

Chapter 2

Daily Telegraph 4 March 1999.
Helsinki Sanormat 20 March 1999.
The Times 10 June 1991.
BBC PM programme 19 April 1999.
Edward Ludbrook, *The Big Picture*, Legacy Communications.

Chapter 3

Mark Greene, *Thank God it's Monday Morning*, Scripture
    Union
Daily Telegraph 24 March 1999.

Chapter 4

Dennis Peacocke, *Almighty and Sons*, Sovereign World
    Books.

Chapter 5

George MacDonald, *The Curate's Awakening*, Bethany House
    Publishing.

Chapter 8

George Eldon Ladd, *The Kingdom of God.* (Out of Print-Publisher – Unknown)

Chapter 9

George MacDonald, *The Curate's Awakening*, Bethany House Publishing
Peter Wagner, *Your Spiritual Gifts Can Help Your Church Grow*, Regal Books

Chapter 10

Charles Kingsley, *Life Letters*, Out of print.
Ralph L. Lewis & Gregg Lewis, *Learning To Preach Like Jesus*, Crossway Books.
Derek Kidner, *Proverbs*, (page 24), IVP.

Chapter 13

ETHOS communications, *Ethos – Ethics In Business.*

TOPICS FOR PREACHING AND TEACHING

Here is a list of ideas for church leaders and housegroup leaders. It is not exhaustive but might give some starting points.

At a recent 'Ultimate Intentions' weekend, Paul Williams and Julian Sayer facilitated a small group session on 'the workplace'. Seventy people turned up and the group was split up into six smaller groups for discussion.

What follows is the outcome of those discussions summarised in no particular order and taken from a flip chart!

Lack of fellowship
Management persecution
People expect more
Increased pressure – customers/employers
Honour employers
Workplace as a 'that'
Making time for relationships – difficult
Finding time to listen to God for wisdom/help
Excellence – people really notice and watch you!
Boldness/fear
How do you set out your stall?
Need to hear others' testimonies
Attitude towards others – learning to love them

How much to join in with the social side?
Recognising and responding to bad deals

A fabulous book in helping any church leader to preach with relevance is *Learning To Preach Like Jesus* by Ralph Lewis and Gregg Lewis (Crossway Books ISBN 0-89107-536-4)

Appendix VI

FOUNDATIONS FOR A BUSINESS

1. Always giving the customer specifically what they want and then some more.

- the product itself
- every detail relating to service

2. Every dealing a customer has with us should be a pleasant experience every time, at every level of contact, whatever the reason for contact.

- easy to ask
- overall situation
- activity going on
- specific area
- service involved

3. To spot undeveloped, or even unknown, skills, talents or contributions in people and to open doors of opportunity for those people. Often we accept that these individuals will not know what lies within themselves – it may well be latent or dormant.

4. Unity of all staff

- sales & research
- recreational principles
- social policy
- a pro-active form of communication

5. Motivation to be clear
In the salt mine each miner was given a precious commodity in the form of salt each week which they were allowed to dispose of any way they saw fit. Art and culture formed an important part of the total environment.

6. Responsibility

7. Nothing fake, everything real

8. Good treatment of animals and men. The horses were winched to the surface one month in three and were put out to graze after ten years

9. Longevity

10. A transcendent cause

These foundations were conceived after a visit to the Wieliczka salt mine, stimulated by the observations made.

SERVICES AND RESOURCES FROM DAVID OLIVER FOR CHURCHES AND BUSINESSES

Business services

Forget the cold call – appointment generation on tap, marketing audits and one day clinics

Customised in-house and highly tailored training in

- sales
- negotiation
- customer care
- leadership development

Training packs on

- Developing powerful questions and handling objections
- Direct mail faxshots and advertising that works

Churches

If you are interested in organising a one day event with David Oliver please call to discuss.

Leaders resource pack

Includes study guide and ten workbooks for church related groups. £45 per pack

Fax orders or enquiries now on 01256 895882 or call 01256 895529 or email insightmarketing@btinternet.com

Address:
Insight Marketing
Lynch Hill Park
Whitchurch
RG24 7NF